Bollywood Crafts

20 projects inspired
by popular Indian cinema

Momtaz Begum-Hossain

THE GUILD OF MASTER CRAFTSMAN
PUBLICATIONS

GUILD OF MASTER
CRAFTSMAN PUBLICATIONS

Bollywood Crafts

20 projects inspired
by popular Indian cinema

Momtaz Begum-Hossain

GUILD OF MASTER
CRAFTSMAN PUBLICATIONS

145.5
BEG

First published 2006 by

Guild of Master Craftsman Publications Ltd

Castle Place, 166 High Street, Lewes,
East Sussex, BN7 1XU

Text © Momtaz Begum-Hossain 2006
© in the Work GMC Publications 2006

Photographs by Anthony Bailey

ISBN-13 978-1-86108-418-7
ISBN-10 1-86108-418-8

The publisher and author can accept no legal
responsibility for any consequences arising
from the application of information, advice or
instructions given in this publication.

Whilst every effort has been made to obtain
permission from the copyright holders for all
material used in this book, the publishers will
be pleased to hear from anyone who has not
been appropriately acknowledged, and to make
the correction in future reprints.

A catalogue record of this book is available
from the British Library.

Production Manager: Hilary MacCallum
Managing Editor: Gerrie Purcell
Project Editor: Dominique Page
Managing Art Editor: Gilda Pacitti
Designer: Rebecca Mothersole

Set in Eurostile and Bauhaus
Colour origination by MRM Graphics
Printed and bound in Singapore
by Kyodo Printing Co.

**I would like to dedicate this book
to the memory of my mother, Rehana Begum,
who will always be my biggest inspiration.**

Contents

Introduction   8

The Films & Projects

Awara   15
  Silver Mirror   19
  Sari Bedspread   23

Mughal-E-Azam   27
  Photo Frame   31
  Gold Pot   35

Jewel Thief   39
  Brooches   43
  Trinket Boxes   47

Caravan   51
  Lamp   53
  Cushion   59

Bobby   63
  Bindi Greeting Card   65
  Sandals   69

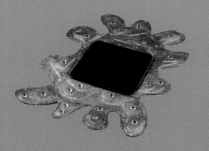

Umrao Jaan   73
Belt   75
Money Purse   79

Roop Ki Rani Choron Ka Raja   83
Handbag   85
Notebooks   89

Khabi Khushi Khabi Gham   93
Celebration Bowl   97
Vase   101

Devdas   105
Candles   109
Placemats   115

Koi Mil Gaya   119
Bolster Cushion   121
Canvas Artwork   125

Project Preparation
Materials   130
Equipment   138
Techniques   142
Safety Notes   146

Suppliers   148
Further Recommended Viewing   152
Acknowledgements   154
About the Author   155
Index   156

Introduction

The idea for *Bollywood Crafts* came to me one Sunday afternoon as I sat in a samosa house in Southall, West London. I had spent the morning scouring the stalls for the latest Bollywood soundtrack CDs and window-shopping at the many Indian clothing boutiques.

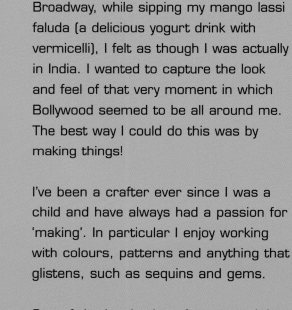

I was so blown away by all the colours and designs in the shops and on the streets that looking outside at the busy Broadway, while sipping my mango lassi faluda (a delicious yogurt drink with vermicelli), I felt as though I was actually in India. I wanted to capture the look and feel of that very moment in which Bollywood seemed to be all around me. The best way I could do this was by making things!

I've been a crafter ever since I was a child and have always had a passion for 'making'. In particular I enjoy working with colours, patterns and anything that glistens, such as sequins and gems.

One of the inspirations for my work is Bollywood films. I don't think I've ever watched a movie without being amazed by the style and fashion. While some people are mesmerised by the stories, songs and choreography, it's always the 'look' of the film that excites me. Whether it's the colourful costumes, the artistic editing or breathtaking shot composition, there's usually an element of style that has the 'wow' factor. This book shows you how easy it is to adopt this Indian movie look into everyday craft projects. They are inspired by what I consider to be the ten most stylish Bollywood movies made between the 1950s and the new millennium. It starts with *Awara* (1951), a classic black and white drama, then journeys through the decades to include movies from the swinging sixties where Bollywood was influenced by London fashions, and ends with the children's movie *Koi Mil Gaya* (2003), the first ever sci-fi Bollywood production. These changing Bollywood styles over the decades will be explored through crafts.

Whether you want to make something for your home or as a gift, the projects are suitable for the absolute beginner but I hope experienced crafters will also find ideas and inspiration. Techniques are varied and include sewing, painting and collage work – but don't be afraid if any of these are new to you, as they have been designed for anyone to have a go. If you are new to crafting you'll soon discover that as a hobby it can become very addictive! Making your own things is really fun, and best of all there are no rules. This is one of the things I like most about crafting. It's all about you – choosing colours and materials that you want, finding inspiration as it grabs you and producing one-off pieces that have the personal touch. You don't need to spend a lot of money either. All you need is a basic kit of craft materials. Whether you enjoy exploring haberdashery stores or cutting up old clothes to get fabrics, it's always possible to be a budget crafter.

I hope you will enjoy my book, whether you choose to make one of the featured projects or adapt them to suit your own tastes. I also hope you'll watch the movies they are inspired by. Before you start, though, overleaf are some Bollywood facts to set the scene.

Bollywood Film Facts

Bollywood is the biggest film industry in the world. Approximately one thousand films are made in India under the 'Bollywood' umbrella each year (that is double the amount of Hollywood films) and over 12 million Indians watch a Bollywood film every day. The films are also popular throughout the Middle East, Russia and Africa, and, increasingly, Western audiences are surrendering to the charms of Indian cinema.

Bollywood is also referred to as Hindi cinema – there are 22 official languages spoken in India; however, the major movies are made in Hindi as it is the country's dominant language, though films in other languages, such as Tamil and Urdu, are also made. Although the main hub of production companies are based in Mumbai (Bombay), films are shot in locations all over the country and recent films have even been set abroad.

Like mainstream Hollywood movies, Bollywood films also fall into specific genres, such as action or romance, but most are multi-genre, family movies. In India, going to the movies is a family event, and often several generations watch a film together. This means the content has to appeal to all. It also

means filmmakers have to be creative in their approach to telling narratives. How they express emotions is a key element. Emotions are represented not just through acting, but also through the use of spectacle – songs and dance.

The key to a successful movie is to have a popular soundtrack, and for the choreography that accompanies it to be equally impressive. Song sequences usually start in the middle of a dialogue and are a break from the reality of the storyline. Characters are transported to different locations and their costumes become very significant; a leading lady can go through several costume changes per dance scene, which makes for compelling viewing! When you're watching a song from a film, it's best to ignore the subtitles and instead let yourself be entertained by the visuals. The choreography is a mixture of Indian dancing styles with global influences such as MTV. Extras play a key role in bringing the dances to life, and as a viewer at the cinema, I often want to get up and join in!

Some Bollywood films are inspired by Hollywood tales, but most are original ideas, often based on moral or family dilemmas. Like Hollywood, the star system is an important aspect of

Bollywood and the biggest actors and actresses are celebrities in their own right. Unlike Hollywood, however, Indian actors often work on several films at one time, even switching between movie sets in the same day. And while Hollywood left behind its musicals in the 1950s, Bollywood films always contain a performance element. Actors have to demonstrate impeccable dancing skills as well as acting ability.

If you have yet to watch a Bollywood movie, don't worry! They are far more accessible than you may think, with cinemas and rental stores responding to audience demands by showing or stocking new movies. Don't be alarmed by the length; Bollywood movies are longer than other films to allow for the songs, but there is always an interval. If you're already a convert, hopefully you'll agree with the films I've selected; though of course, there are many more that could have a made the shortlist – some of these are listed on pages 152–153.

Bollywood films are an exciting and original contribution to the filmmaking world and, as the popularity of Bollywood continues to spread around the globe, Indian filmmakers are getting more progressive with their plots, special effects and visuals. This means that films will develop stylistically even further and continue to get better – something I'm really looking forward to!

The films
& Projects

1951

Awara

Directed by Raj Kapoor

Awara is the only black and white film to feature in this collection. It follows the life of Raju, a petty thief who is reacquainted with his childhood school friend, Rita, who has grown up to be a lawyer. Raju falls in love with Rita but his reputation means he is socially excluded and eventually charged with attempted murder of her guardian, the renowned judge Raghunath, who, it turns out, is also Raju's father.

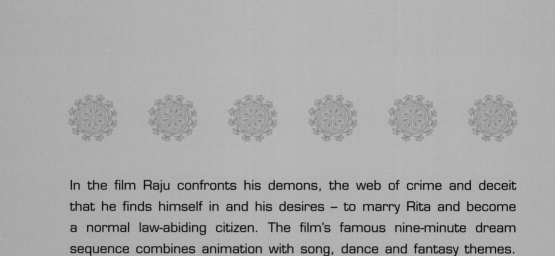

In the film Raju confronts his demons, the web of crime and deceit that he finds himself in and his desires – to marry Rita and become a normal law-abiding citizen. The film's famous nine-minute dream sequence combines animation with song, dance and fantasy themes. It features monsters, gods, large puppets and a beautiful spiral staircase. The dream plays on manifestations of heaven and hell as

seen through the eyes of the protagonist, Raju. The shape and design of the mirror on page 19 is inspired by the dream's spectacular architectural features.

As this is such a classic movie, for the second project I decided to take something classically Indian and give it a new function, so I have converted a full-size sari into a convenient bedspread or throw. It provides a good introduction to using fabric, as it doesn't require any sewing!

star fact

After the success of *Awara*, the two lead stars, Raj Kapoor and Nargis, worked exclusively together; in the five years that followed they starred in ten romantic movies together.

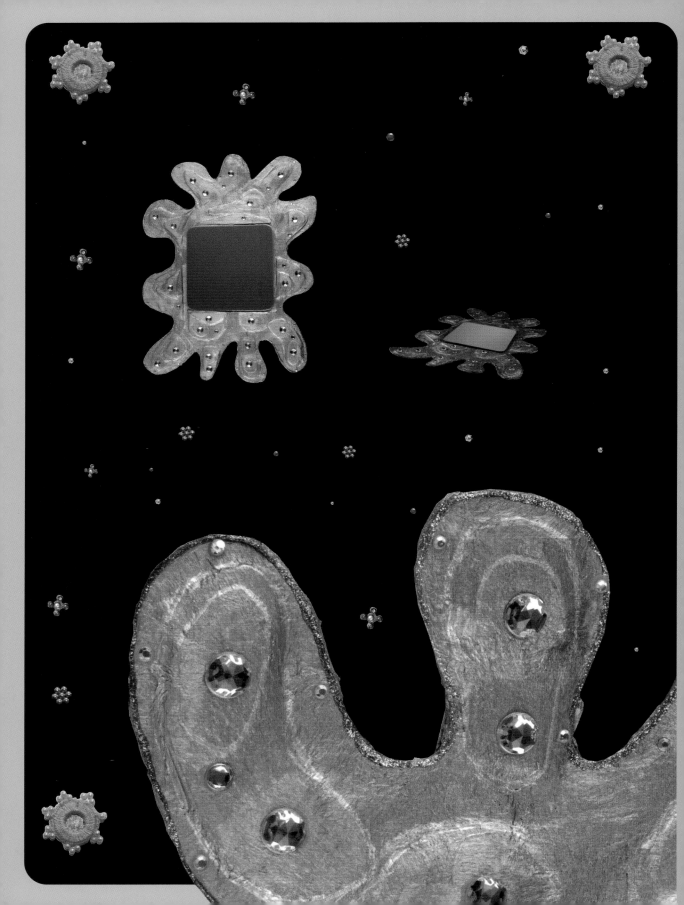

Silver Mirror

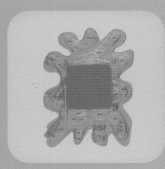

Hang this silver papier-mâché mirror in your hallway or staircase; it acts both as a mirror and a piece of artwork in its own right.

You will need:

Materials
- A small flat mirror
- One A2 (42 x 59.4cm) sheet of thick card
- Scraps of corrugated card
- White crepe paper
- PVA glue
- Strong glue
- Silver acrylic paint and glitter paint
- Clear acrylic stones in small medium and large sizes
- Picture-hanging fixture
- Pencil

Equipment
- Cutting mat
- Craft knife
- Paintbrush to apply glue

Making the mirror

1 Draw a large freehand shape with a curvy border onto a sheet of thick card. Cut it out using the craft knife and the cutting mat. 🖤

2 Place the mirror in the centre of the shape and draw around it in pencil to show where it will later be glued. 🖤

3 Use scraps of card and corrugated card to cut out the shapes that will become the 3D patterns on the mirror frame. Draw these freehand yourself.

4 Glue the shapes randomly onto the card base, avoiding the pencil lines that mark the position of the mirror. Leave to dry. 🖤

5 Mix a paste of ⅓ water and ⅔ PVA. Tear the tissue paper into pieces, dip in the glue mixture and stick over the frame. When dry, cover the rest of the frame in the same way and use a paintbrush to ensure that there are no bumps and that the 3D areas have been properly covered. Cover the back of the frame in tissue too, then paint the whole side silver. 🖤

6 Paint the frame silver and edge it in silver glitter paint.

7 Glue small gemstones around the edge and medium and large stones in the raised shapes on the mirror. Outline these shapes using a silver marker pen. 🖤

8 Glue the mirror in the centre of the space with strong glue. When it is dry, attach a picture-hanging fixture at the back so that you can hang your mirror on the wall. 🖤

Tips

✹ Use the leftover card from the sheet that you cut the main mirror frame from for some of the 3D areas. Many of the edges have already been curved and shaped so they will fit on the mirror frame well.

✹ You could paint the frame any colour to suit your own home furnishings.

star fact

As well as playing Raju, Raj Kapoor also produced and directed the movie, and many others, from the 1940s right through to the 1980s.

Sari Bedspread

This is a simple way to convert a sari into a furnishing to brighten up any interior. Once it has been cut to size and prevented from fraying, the sari becomes a suitable throw for your bedroom or living room.

You will need:

Materials
- A sari of your choice
- Fusible webbing/iron-on hemming

Equipment
- Fabric scissors
- Iron and ironing board
- Clean tea towel

Sizing up the throw

1 To make a single bedspread, cut the sari in half through the longest edge so that you have two pieces that are the same size.

2 To make a double bedspread, join the two pieces together along the opposite edge to that which you cut.

Using fusible webbing

This is the no-sew method that can be used to secure hems onto lightweight fabrics and ensures the sari doesn't fray. Two sides of the sari fabric will not require a hem but the side you have just cut and the opposite end will.

3 To make the hem, place your sari on an ironing board and make a 1in (2.5cm) fold along the edge of the fabric. Cut a length of fusible webbing the same length as the hem or small pieces that can be placed beside each other. Put the webbing inside the hem fold. **Ⓐ**

4 Place a tea towel on top of the fold. Iron over the tea towel using an even pressure for five to eight seconds, until the webbing bonds the hem together; it acts as a glue and sticks the hem in place permanently. Do this along the entire length of the hemline and then repeat on the other side. **Ⓑ**

Tips

✹ A sari can be converted into any kind of throw, whether it's for a bed, sofa or anywhere else in your home.

✹ This technique is also suited to neatening any type of thin fabric.

✹ If you have pinking shears, use these to cut the sari instead of fabric scissors, as it will ensure a neater edge with no frays before you make your hem.

5 When making a double bedspread, join the two pieces using fusible webbing. Overlap one on top of the other and fold both edges together to obtain a neat join.

chorus

Awaara Hoon, Ya Gardish Mein Hoon
Aasman Ka Tara Hoon
Awaara Hoon...

**I'm a tramp,
Whether I'm rising or falling
I'm always a star...**

1961

Mughal-E-Azam

Directed by K. Asif

(re-released in full colour 2005)

The setting and location for this film is breathtaking. It was originally made in black and white with just one scene in the film, a dance, filmed in colour. However, 44 years after it was released the entire film was restored in full colour.

It is an epic tale about pride, honour and the duties faced by the Great Mughal Emperor Akbar, who forbids his son, Prince Salim, to marry a poor maid, Anarkali, with whom he is deeply in love.

The opulence of the film is apparent in the fine details of the background, which are seen in every scene of the film, and this explains why the film originally took nine years to complete.

The regal glitz of the Emperor's palace is represented by the sequin-coated photo frame on page 31. I wanted to recreate the luxury of the magnificent location in the cheapest way possible. I really like how the sequins catch the light when the frame is put by a window on a sunny afternoon.

The second project is a gold-painted ceramic pot that has been decorated in a 'cheat's mosaic' style by gluing on lots of small diamond-shaped and round shisha mirrors. I wanted to create something for the home that would be like owning an ornament from the palace. The use of so many mirrors also represents a scene in the film where Anarkali dances and the screen is split many times to create a kaleidoscope effect. This is the scene that was originally shot in full colour.

Photo Frame

Place your frame on your window as an ornament so that it catches the sunlight; it will reflect the colours onto your walls, making your room feel like a royal palace.

You will need:

Materials
- Wooden photo frame
- PVA glue
- Fine pink glitter
- Small holographic round sequins
- Round gold sequins
- Pink and gold seed beads
- Gems (optional)
- Red bugle beads (optional)
- Sticky motifs
- Pink emulsion or acrylic paint

Equipment
- Glue spreader
- Cocktail sticks
- Paintbrush

Preparing the background

1 Remove the inner glass and backing card and paint the surface of the wooden frame pink. Ⓐ

Decorating the frame

2 Work in small areas; do not cover the whole frame with glue in one go. Start at one section and apply a thick layer of PVA glue with your spreader. Sprinkle the small sequins on and spread them out using a cocktail stick. Now add some of the large gold sequins. Your sequins do not need to be totally flat – they will also stick if their sides touch the surface of the glue. Next add gold and pink seed beads. Ⓑ

3 If you want, you could add gems and bugle beads among the sequins – they will add details but won't stand out as the sequins have more of an impact on the design. When you have filled all the gaps with sequins, sprinkle on fine glitter using your fingers – this will mean your frame sparkles but doesn't look overly heavy with glitter. Ⓒ

4 Decorate the rest of the frame, working in small sections at a time.

5 Stick a motif in each of the four corners and one on each side. Leave the frame to dry. Ⓓ

Finishing touches

6 Once dry, you may find some of the sequins fall off. Fill in any gaps by applying glue and glitter with a small paintbrush.

Tips

❁ Work in sections rather than covering the whole frame so that the glue doesn't dry out. You need to cover the frame with sequins and glitter while the glue is still wet. If you cover the frame in one go, by the time you reach the glitter stage, it may not stick.

❁ The crystallized effect created by this technique can be used for decorating many other items with flat surfaces – why not try it on a small wooden box or rectangular wooden vase?

chorus

Pyaar kiyaa to darnaa kyaa
Jab pyaar kiyaa to darnaa kyaa

**When one has loved,
Why should one be afraid?**

Gold Pot

Create an original ornament or plant pot with this very simple mosaic-inspired technique.

You will need:

Materials

- A large ceramic pot
- White emulsion paint
- Gold acrylic paint
- Diamond-shaped shisha mirrors
- Round shisha foils and borders
- Mosaic glue
- Pencil

Equipment

- Cocktail stick
- Paintbrush

Preparing the pot

1 Paint the entire pot white; this will create a good undercoat before you apply the gold paint.

2 When dry, paint over the white layer with the gold acrylic paint.

Decorating the pot

3 With your pencil, make small marks 1in (2.5cm) apart in diagonal lines down the sides of the pot. **A**

4 You will be gluing alternate lines of diamond and round shisha mirrors. To do this use a cocktail stick to apply a small amount of mosaic glue in the centre back of each mirror and then press in place where your pencil mark is. **B**

5 Continue to do this all over the surface of the pot. Do not glue the entire surface of the shisha mirror as the glue will seep out at the side. **C**

Tips

This project is referred to as using mosaic techniques, but it is not actual mosaic. Mosaics require grouting which involves filling up the spaces between the mirrors and making the surface even. It requires a lot of time but gives a fantastic result. This pot is based on mosaics by creating a 3D effect using small mirrors that are similar to tiles.

When using a cocktail stick to apply glue, start by pouring the glue into a small palette or bowl and dip the cocktail stick in it. Use one end as the glue applicator and the dry end as a tool to poke the embellishments into place.

1967

Jewel Thief

Directed by Vijay Anand

Jewel Thief is a classic cult movie that helped to determine the look and fashions of late sixties Hindi cinema. With its retro musical sounds and choreography, and ingredients such as Cadillac car chases and huge sixties sunglasses, it echoes the fashion and style of what was happening in the West during the decade. It's easy to forget the viewer is watching an Indian film, since so much of it seems American.

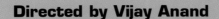

The plot is not just a tale of jewel theft, but identity theft – as the protagonist, Vinay (Dev Anand), discovers. He is continuously mistaken for a notorious jewel thief called Amar and spends the whole film trying to discover the identity of the mysterious Amar.

The fashion, architecture and designs in the film have a strong sixties flavour. This was the decade that Indian cinema fell in love with colour, and by the end of the sixties most Hindi films were made in full colour, adding depth and excitement to the visual aspects of the films. *Jewel Thief* took full advantage of this but also found imaginative ways to add mystery and suspense to the plot by creating modern sets with moving walls, modern light fixtures and hidden corridors. But contemporary style remained the main focus of the films; in one party scene in particular, the setting is awash with colour. None of the walls are the same, all are made of different patterns and textures, and I have adopted this idea for the trinket boxes on page 47. They are made of different coloured fabrics, trims and motifs. The brooches on page 43, however, are inspired by the jewellery shop in the film. They are a really easy way to make use of gemstones and sequins and can be worn on bags or jacket lapels.

Brooches

Transform plain badges with multi-coloured stones and gems to create eye-catching bejewelled brooches.

You will need:

Materials

- A selection of round sequins, seed beads, gems and Swarovski crystals
- Badges
- Strong craft glue

Equipment

- Glue applicator
- Cocktail sticks

For the pin badge

1 Apply glue using a cocktail stick all around the edge of the pin badge. Place sequins all around this edge.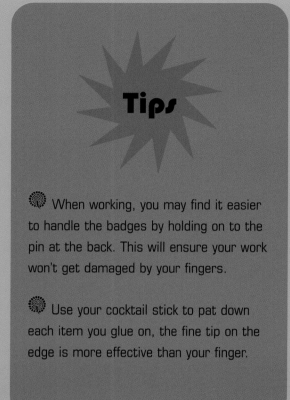

2 Glue a seed bead in the centre of each sequin. Glue a larger sequin in the centre and place a Swarovski crystal in the middle.

3 Now glue sequins in the space between the edge and the centre.

4 Finally, glue a gem on top of each sequin and top with a small Swarovski crystal.

For the giant badge

1 Take a large birthday badge and choose a big centrepiece, such as an Indian motif.

2 Cut a circle of felt and glue it in the centre of the badge before you start; this will make covering up the original design easier.

3 Make in the same way as for the pin badge. Apply rows of sequins and add gems, crystals and beads according to your own design and in colours of your choice (see picture on page 42 for ideas).

Tips

❀ When working, you may find it easier to handle the badges by holding on to the pin at the back. This will ensure your work won't get damaged by your fingers.

❀ Use your cocktail stick to pat down each item you glue on, the fine tip on the edge is more effective than your finger.

Trinket Boxes

Use these fabric-covered boxes to store your own jewels and treasures. They are also perfect for placing gifts in or make a great addition to your home when stacked together for storing small odds and ends.

You will need:

Materials
* 5 x 2½in (12.75 x 6.5cm) cardboard gift box with lid
* Craft foam
* Fabrics of your choice
* Double-sided tape
* Trims and motifs of your choice
* Pencil

Equipment
* Fabric scissors
* Ruler

No sewing
required!

Covering the lid

1 Cut a square of foam the same size as the lid and stick it on top. **(A)**

2 Place the lid face downwards on top of a 10½ x 10½in (27 x 27cm) square of fabric.

3 Stick the lid in the centre of the fabric using strips of double-sided tape.

4 Fold in two opposite ends of fabric and tape in place. **(B)**

5 For the two remaining sides, fold in the edges to create a large triangular shape as if you were wrapping a present. Fold over the inside edge of the lid and tape in place. As you stick each side down, hold the fabric as taut as possible to prevent air getting trapped. **(C)**

6 To cover the inside of the lid you need a square of foam that is a little smaller than the lid. Stick the foam onto a 6in (15.5cm) square of fabric and fold in the edges so that one side is covered. Stick this directly inside the lid. **(D)**

7 Make two more fabric-covered foam rectangles and stick on top of the two sides of the lid that were folded in last. **(E)**

Covering the base

8 Cut a 15½in (40cm) square from your chosen fabric. Place the bottom of the box in the centre of the fabric and stick it down using double-sided tape; make sure that you stick down the middle so as to prevent air from getting trapped.

9 As you did for the lid, fold in two opposite corners and stick them down. For the remaining two corners, fold them into triangles as if you were wrapping a present, fold these over the inside edges of the box and stick them down. You may need to trim off sections of unwanted fabric so that the edges are less bulky. **(F)**

10 As you did for the inside of the lid, cut a square of foam a little smaller than the base of the box and two rectangles of foam to become sides. Cover each of these in fabric and glue inside the base. **(G)**

Finishing touches

11 Stick trims of your choice along the sides and bottom of the box – don't place them too high up or the box will not close. **(H)**

12 Stick motifs of your choice in the centre of the lid. **(I)**

1971

Caravan

Directed by Nasir Hussain

Caravan is a thrilling adventure that is full of twists and turns. Suneeta is a young woman who discovers her father has been murdered and she will be next, so she fakes her own death and hides away with a group of travelling Romanies.

She falls in love with the travelling troupe's van driver and although there is a happy ending, she faces many obstacles including kidnap, abduction and escaping murder on several occasions before they can settle down.

The costumes in *Caravan* are stunning and give a strong visual representation of Indian folk style. Dresses are incredibly colourful with patterns and designs. Rather than basing the projects on the clothes worn by the two main protagonists, I have based them on the costumes worn by the background extras in the film, many of whom don't speak but their presence has a huge impact on the film's style.

I have designed a lampshade and matching cushion set that takes influence from the costumes worn by the Romani community.

Lamp

Customising a lamp is a simple way to update your living space.

You will need:

Materials

- A canvas lampshade
- Orange printed cotton fabric and matching thread
- Orange and black tapestry (or other thick) yarn
- Two lengths of trim
- Gold bias binding/gold trim
- Double-sided tape
- Shisha mirror foils and borders
- Red and black wooden beads
- Red acrylic stones
- Fabric glue

Equipment

- Scissors
- One large darning needle
- One ordinary thread needle

Covering the lamp

1 You won't be able to cover the shade with one single piece of fabric as it won't fit evenly around the curves of the shade. Instead you need to cut three rectangles of fabric that each measure just over a third of the lamp's surface in width, and are slightly wider towards the bottom to match the shape of the lampshade. Lengthwise there should be an extra inch (2.5cm) of seam allowance at each end. **A**

2 Fold your first piece of fabric in half lengthways and stretch it vertically across the lampshade from top to bottom. Now hand-stitch down the raw edge of the fabric (fold over the edge to neaten) so it attaches to the shade. Fold over the top end inside the top of the shade and fold the bottom end over the bottom edge and stitch them in place. **B**

3 Attach the second piece of fabric in the same way – start attaching from one edge of the first piece. Again, fold in the two edges at the top and bottom and stitch in place. Two thirds of the shade will be covered. You now need to attach the final third in the same way as the two other pieces. **C**

star fact

Supporting actress Aruni Irani, who plays Nisha, has starred in over 300 Bollywood movies. She was admired for her dancing ability and still makes appearances today.

Adding details

4 Glue a trim around the centre of the shade and another at the top. The easiest way to glue the trims is to paste down sections at a time rather than wetting it all at once, as this may create air bubbles. Smooth these out as you go along and remember to keep pulling the trim tight so that it sticks in a straight line around the shade. **D**

5 To neaten the top edge, attach the gold bias binding or gold trim over the top rim of the shade using the double-sided tape.

6 Stick some red gemstones randomly on the shade or pick out shapes on the fabric print and place appropriately. Glue on some shisha mirrors if you wish. **E**

chorus

Piya tu ab to aa jaa
Shola sa mann daheke, aake
bujha jaa

My love come to me
Put out this fire that rages
within me

Making the tassels

7 Cut out a rectangle of card that measures 8 x 2in (20 x 5cm) and fold it in half.

8 Wind the orange yarn around it 20 times and then cut the yarn off.

9 Wind on ten layers of the black yarn.

10 Take a small length of orange yarn and pass it through the top end of the layers of yarn then tie a knot.

11 Cut through the bottom edge of the yarn so that the whole piece comes away from the card. Fluff it up so that the two yarns mix.

12 Cut a small piece of orange yarn and wrap it around several times approximately ¾in (2cm) down from the top of the tassel then tie it firmly and trim the excess.

13 Now trim the tassels so that they are even in length.

14 Using the darning needle, make holes along the bottom of the shade at equal distances.

15 Thread three wooden beads on to one end of the hanging threads at the top of the tassel. Next thread it through a hole in the shade and pull it as tight as it will go. Tie the two ends in the inside of the shade and trim off the ends to neaten. Hang all your tassels in the same way all along the edge of the shade.

star fact

Actress Helen, who plays Monica, was known as Bollywood's answer to Marilyn Monroe. She was renowned for her spectacular cabaret performances which included Western-inspired choreography.

Cushion

Make a set of these small cushions to accompany your dining chairs, or snuggle up to them on the sofa as you melt into a movie.

You will need:

Materials

- Felt squares – red, orange, white, black
- 5ft (1.5m) black felt or wool fabric
- Shisha mirrors – four small and one large
- Two trims of your choice
- Cushion filling
- Thread to match the felt
- Pencil

Equipment

- Sewing needle
- Compass
- Scissors
- Ruler

Making the main design

1 Cut out the following shapes from your felt:

Black Two squares (main cushion base): 9½in (25cm). One circle (centre): 4½in (12cm) diameter.

Red Four squares: 1⅓in (3.5cm). Four squares: 2in (5cm). One circle: 2¼in (5.5cm) diameter (centre).

Orange One square (main design base): 8in (20cm). One circle: 2¾in (7cm) diameter (centre).

White Four squares (corners): 2in (5cm). Ten white triangles: the two sides should measure 1¾6in (3cm) and the bottom 1in (2.5cm) but it needs to have a curved edge so that it fits inside the black circle and around the edge of the orange circle. **A**

2 Start by stitching together the layers that are not directly stitched onto the orange square, such as the black centre circle. (Use the prick-stitch method shown on page 144.) Stitch the orange circle onto the black circle then stitch the white triangles around the orange circle. **B**

3 Next stitch the red circle inside the orange circle and then add the large shisha mirror in the centre. The whole motif can now be stitched in the centre of the orange square.

4 To make the corner motifs, stitch the small red squares inside the white squares and place shisha mirrors in the centre. These can then be stitched into the four corners of the square. Cut the 2in (5cm) red squares in half to form two triangles and stitch these at the two sides of the white squares to complete the design. **C**

5 Stitch the whole orange square into one of the large black squares in the centre. Stitch trims along the edges of the square using running stitch (see page 144).

6 Pin and tack the two black squares together along three sides with the facing sides together. Sew each of the three sides using a sewing machine or running stitch, and for the fourth side stitch up the ends leaving a gap in the middle so that you have a pocket.

7 Turn the cushion inside out so that the main motif is visible and then stuff it with filling. Push out any air and make sure the filling looks smooth and even.

8 When you are happy with the height and feel of the cushion, finish it by hand-stitching together the remaining opening. **D**

chorus

Daiya hey main yeh kahan aa phasi
Hey re phasi kaise phasi
Rona aave na aave hasi
Pape bachalo tushi

**What a mess I've got myself into
How did I land in it?
I can neither laugh nor cry
Save me someone**

1973

Bobby

Directed by Raj Kapoor

Stylish and modern are two words to describe what became known as the ultimate teenage Bollywood film. Bobby, played by 14-year-old Dimple Kapadia, is the feisty heroine of the movie who elopes with her boyfriend Raja. The film's Western-inspired fashion really caught the imaginations of Indian youth. Mini skirts, bikinis and flowing scarves, as worn by Bobby, were adopted by fashion-conscious teenage viewers.

Teenage male viewers, on the other hand, were mesmerised by the cool scooter driven by Raja, who is played by Rishi Kapoor, the 18-year-old son of the director. The two teenagers embark on an adolescent adventure, experiencing the highs and lows of teenage love. Although their story isn't always a happy one, there are substantial comical elements to make this an entertaining, family movie.

Bobby is an example of the fusing of East and West styles, which is an increasingly common theme in Bollywood. The two projects that follow take inspiration from Bobby by taking something Western and giving it a glamorous Bollywood makeover.

Bindi Greeting Card

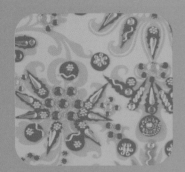

This is a fun way to transform a Western-style printed greeting card into a new design that really speaks East/West. It gives you the opportunity to play with colours, shapes and patterns and you can never go wrong – each attempt is unique and looks amazing!

You will need:

Materials
- A card/design/print/postcard of your choice
- Bindis
- Sparkle stickers (optional)

Equipment
- Scissors (optional)

Embellishing the card

1 Take your chosen printed design.

2 Begin to embellish your design with pretty stickers or bindis. If your image has shapes, such as curves or bends, like the card here, try and fit your bindis inside the shapes to complement them. **B**

3 Continue until you are happy with the design. Remember, there are no real rules for what you should do as it depends on your chosen image. **C**

Get sticking!

Tips

✺ Look for a patterned postcard, gift card, wrapping paper or poster with interesting shapes or designs.

✺ Be colourful – add as much colour as possible to create a card that's bold, bright and really appealing. Remember, it doesn't need to remain a card, you could mount it in a frame and admire it on your walls.

✺ You may find it helps taking sections of stickers or bindis, in which case you can cut them down to your own requirements.

✺ Duplicate – make your own shapes, such as semi-circles, using bindis or stickers and see how many times you can duplicate this design on your card.

chorus

Main shaayar to nahin, magar ae haseen
Jab se dekha maine tujhko
Mujhko shaayari aa gayi, main shaayar to nahin…

**I'm no poet, but my pretty one
Ever since I've seen you,
poetry has come to me…**

Sandals

When you're as stylish as Bobby, new shoes are a must. This pair takes inspiration from her unique style, using retro shapes and modern materials. They are great for partying in!

You will need:

Materials
- Wedge sandals with toe posts
- Acrylic paints in blue and green
- Small round gemstones in green and lilac
- Turquoise teardrop gemstones with holes
- Large blue acrylic stones
- Blue craft wire
- Blue 3D paint
- Blue sequin trim
- Blue felt
- Blue marabou trim
- Sequins
- Blue thread
- Pencil
- Superglue

Equipment
- Paintbrushes
- Needle
- Scissors

Painting the wedges

1 Paint the entire surface of the wedge using blue acrylic paint. Ⓐ

2 With a pencil, freehand draw some retro-looking oval shapes on to the wedge and then draw a small oval in each centre. Paint the ovals green and outline them using the 3D paint. Ⓑ

3 Stick the green and purple gemstones in the green section. Ⓒ

4 To neaten the edge where the sole meets the wedge, use superglue to stick on sequin trim all around. Ⓓ

Hanging the beads

5 Cut small pieces of craft wire, thread a bead onto one and then wrap it tightly around the upper of the sandal so that you attach a hanging bead. The end of the wire should not be poking out, but wrapped underneath itself. Continue hanging as many beads as you like. Ⓔ

Decorating the centre section

6 If your sandals have a large area that goes over the foot, make a felt-based plaque that can be glued on. Hand-stitch two large acrylic stones down the centre and then stitch single sequins all around the edge and in the remaining spaces. Glue this directly to the sandal. Ⓕ

Finishing touches

7 Finish the sandal by gluing marabou trim inside the upper. This adds a decorative feature and protects against the wire. Ⓖ

Tip

✺ You don't need to find a pair of sandals that are identical to these; the main thing is that they are wedge sandals so that you can have lots of fun customising the surface area of the wedge.

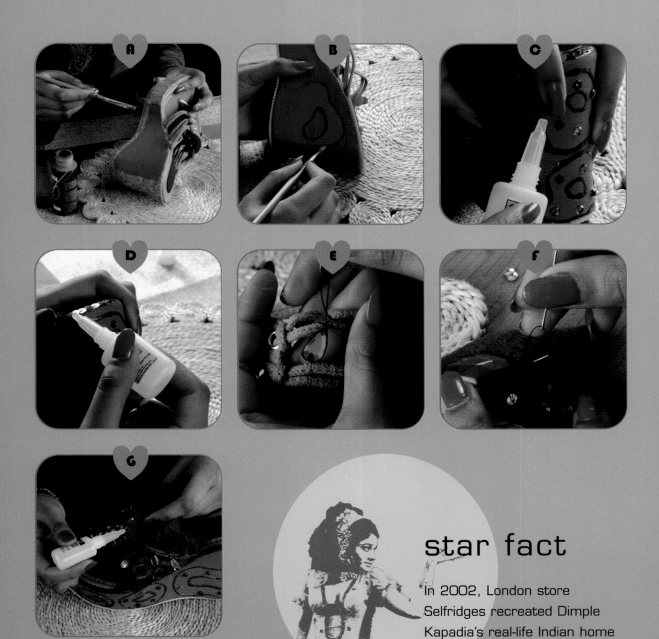

star fact

In 2002, London store Selfridges recreated Dimple Kapadia's real-life Indian home for an exhibition, including her opulent living room and glamorous powder room.

1981

Umrao Jaan

Directed by Muzaffar Ali

The eighties was one of Bollywood's quietest periods in terms of stylish films. Formulaic action movies were in abundance and became the film-goer's diet for the decade. This film is one of the rare eighties gems that broke from the mould. Set in nineteenth-century Lucknow, it follows the story of a girl who gets abducted as a child, is sold to become a courtesan (to provide vocal and dance entertainment for male company) and has her name changed to Umrao Jaan.

She is trained in music and dance and becomes extremely popular among the elite. Despite her popularity, she eventually tries to turn her back on her life as a courtesan and she is also re-united with her long-lost family.

As a courtesan, Umrao Jaan is dressed throughout the movie in the stunning costumes she performs in. The two projects to accompany the film are therefore fashion-based. Using pre-strung sequin trims and a felt base, the neck purse is designed for the character of Umrao to keep her belongings safe while she performs. The mirrored belt is an accessory she could have worn for one of her performances.

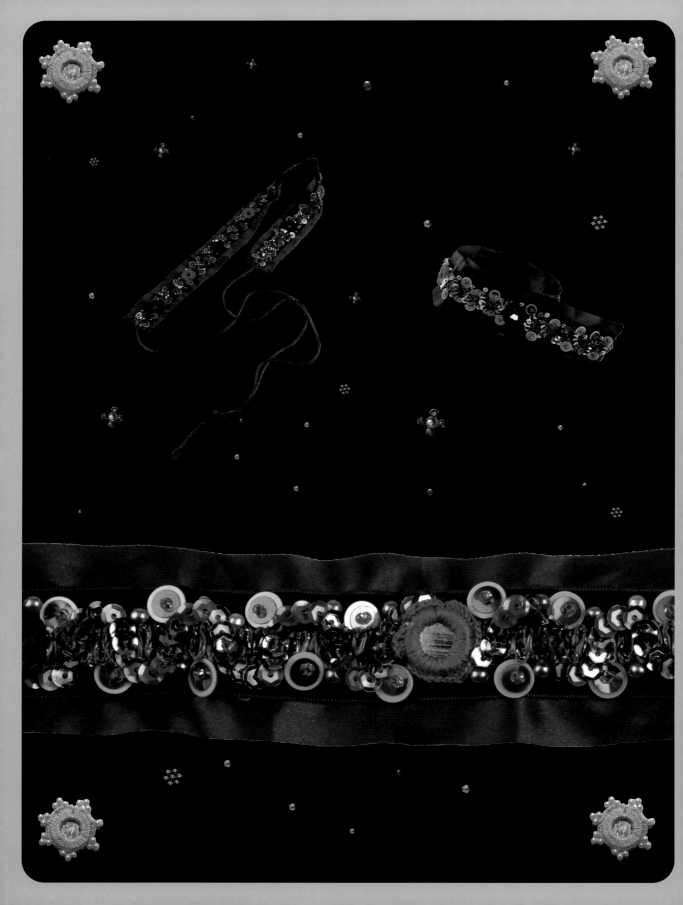

Belt

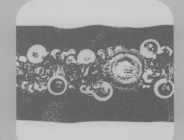

This hand-stitched belt looks like an expensive purchase, but in fact it can be easily stitched while you relax in front of the television.

You will need:

Materials

- Velvet trim in maroon or purple
- Wide maroon ribbon trim
- Trim wider than the velvet but thinner than the ribbon
- 3ft (1m) maroon cord
- Shisha mirrors
- Round sequins in two sizes and two shades of pink
- Pink seed beads
- Small pink pearl beads
- Fabric trim with sequin detail

Equipment

- Needles
- Scissors
- Pins

Tip

Measurements

This belt is one size, the main section measures 21in (53.5cm) and the cords also measure 21in (53.5cm) at each end. If you need to adjust the size, simply decrease or increase the length of the cords.

Decorating the belt

1 Cut a 21in (53.5cm) strip of the velvet trim. Hand-stitch the sequin trim along the centre of the velvet trim. You could pin it in place first to hold it, but as it is so narrow you don't need to tack it. **A**

2 Sew the shisha mirrors at even spaces along the sequin trim. **B**

3 Place the large sequins along both edges of the velvet trim and bring your threaded needle from the reverse of the fabric up through the sequin so that it is secured in place. **C**

4 Thread the needle through the smaller sequins followed by small seed beads so that they sit on top of the larger sequins. **D**

5 Fill in any remaining gaps by sewing on small pink pearly beads.

Assembling the belt

6 Pin the velvet trim along the centre of the ribbon trim, which should be ½in (1.5cm) longer than the velvet trim at each end. Stitch it in place, leaving ½in (1.5cm) unstitched at both ends for you to insert the fastening cord. **E**

7 Cut the 3ft (1m) of cord into two halves. Insert them into the ½in (1.5cm) opening at either end. Hand-stitch this closed, ensuring that a few stitches go through the cord to keep it in place. **F**

Finishing touches

8 To hide the stitches at the back and prevent them from catching on your clothes, cover the back of the ribbon with the remaining trim. Place it across the centre and stitch it in place with a quick running stitch (see page 144) in a similar shade of thread. **G**

9 To neaten the belt, fold the edge of the ribbon that is left after the cord has been inserted to the back and then hand-stitch in place. **H**

Tip

❀ Using an initial trim with sequins on means less work for you, as it will add sequins to your belt without having to individually stitch each one on. However, if you want you could simply hand-stitch on any beads or sequins of your choice or make a belt entirely by couching on sequin trims, a technique used in the next project.

Money Purse

This is a dazzling neck purse that is great for storing loose change and lipgloss!

You will need:

Materials
- Red felt
- Sequin trims in assorted colours of your choice
- Red thread
- A long pre-strung string of small beads
- Pen

Equipment
- Compass
- Needle

Couching the sequins

1 Using a compass, draw and cut out four 4½in (12cm) diameter circles from a piece of red felt.

2 Put two aside; these are for the lining. The other two will become the sides of the purse. On each one, draw a small circle in the centre and then another circle that is half way between the centre circle and the edge of the felt circle. These will act as guides to ensure the circular design remains when you add the sequins.

3 Start by couching (see page 144) the centre section. Place the sequin trim in the centre and couch it down, turning it inwards as you go so that the circle becomes sequin-covered.

4 Couch a second sequin trim on your other line around the circle and then a third around the edge of the circle, without going right to the end.

5 You can now couch the rest of the trims to fill up the surface. Choose different colours or use the same colour twice, like this purse, to create a thicker line of sequins — just continue stitching with the same trim and wind it around as you did in the centre.

6 Repeat what you have done on your second felt circle so that you end up with two identical-looking sequinned circles.

Assembling the purse

7 Hold one finished sequinned side against one of the two remaining plain red circles and stitch them together all the way around using a prick stitch (see page 144). The thickness of the felt means that the stitches won't be seen, so don't worry about being too neat. This is the front of the purse.

8 Make the back in a similar way but rather than joining up the whole circle stitch up just half of it. Place the end of the string of beads into the gap between the sequin and plain side, so that the rest of the necklace creates a long strap for your purse. Sew each protruding strand of the beads securely in place at either side of the gap. When the necklace is secure, you can continue prick stitching up the remaining half of the purse.

9 Finally, sew the front and back together, leaving a gap at the top.

star fact

A remake of *Umrao Jaan* is set to be released in 2006 and stars Bollywood beauty Aishwarya Rai in the lead role.

1993

Roop Ki Rani Choron Ka Raja

Directed by Satish Kaushik

Explosive from start to finish, this is an action-packed Bond-style adventure full of murder, deceit and plenty of stunts.

Simmi and Ramesh meet in an orphanage when they are children – the fathers of both have been murdered by 'Jugran', who can only be described as Bollywood's most evil villain ever. The two are reunited as adults but both have taken on different disguises – Simmi has given herself the alter ego Roop Ki Rani, 'Queen of Beauty', while Ramesh has become known as Choron Ka Raja, 'King of Thieves'. Together they seek their revenge but encounter many obstacles until they unravel the true identity of Jugran.

Roop Ki Rani performs captivating dances throughout the movie in the most fabulous costumes. In the last song of the film, Roop Ki Rani dances in disguise wearing a jewelled, feathered, gold outfit with intricate gold designs and beaded tassel details. The bag and notebook projects that follow take direct inspiration from this dress.

Handbag

Even the plainest of handbags can be dressed up! Using fabrics and trims it's easy to convert an ordinary accessory into a glitzy, glamorous must-have.

You will need:

Materials

- A plain brown fabric handbag
- Gold fabric
- An assortment of gold trims
- Gold ribbon
- Yellow beaded tassel trim
- Yellow feather
- Gold hologram sequin trim
- Shisha mirror rims and foils
- Superglue
- Fabric glue
- Double-sided tape

Equipment

- Scissors
- Plastic gloves

Customizing the bag

1 Cut a piece of gold fabric that fits across most of your bag and, using fabric glue, stick it in place. Do not wet the fabric completely as it will seep through, just line the edges and put a spot in the centre. **A**

2 Glue a thick trim along the bottom edge of the bag all the way along. Do not glue it all at once, attach it in sections instead. **B**

3 Now stick two more trims across the top of the gold fabric and then another trim down the sides. **C**

4 Glue a feather in the centre of the bag and glue a strip of sequin trim along the centre of the feather. **D**

5 Next glue the beaded trim across the top seam of the bag. As it is a heavyweight trim, fabric glue won't be strong enough to hold it, so use a strong superglue. Protect your fingers by wearing a thin pair of plastic gloves. As superglue leaves a residue, use fabric glue to adhere a further gold trim over the edge of the tassel trim to hide the glue marks. **E**

Finishing touches

6 Stick some gold shisha mirrors on the bag.

7 For the bag handle, cut lengths of gold ribbon and stick double-sided tape on one side. Peel off the tape and then wind the trim around the handle. When the length of ribbon runs out, start applying a second length. Wind around the handle at even spaces. **F**

Tips

✵ Making over a bag using glue will only work on a fabric bag, anything more heavyweight, such as leather, will be more difficult to glue.

✵ As the bag is pre-made it is better to glue your embellishments on. If they are sewn on, the stitches will interfere with the bag's lining.

No sewing
required!

Notebooks

You've probably seen fabric-covered notebooks in the shops, but with this method you can add a personal touch by using a material of your choice.

You will need:

Materials
- A hardback notebook
- Fabric of your choice
- Embroidered paper
- Two trims of your choice
- Double-sided tape
- Glue stick

Equipment
- Fabric scissors
- Ruler
- Cocktail stick

Covering the book

1 Lay your book open onto your fabric. Cut around it so that there is a 2in (5cm) gap at the top and bottom edges of the book and a 1½in (4cm) gap at the sides. **A**

2 Starting with the back of the book, place the book open so that the inside cover is facing you. Fold in the right-hand edge of the fabric and glue in place using the glue stick. **B**

3 Make two slits at the top and bottom to separate the book's hinge. **C**

4 At the bottom of the fabric, fold the two outer edges inwards to create triangular shapes then fold the bottom section of fabric upwards, as though wrapping a parcel. Stick in place using double-sided tape. When you are sticking sides down, always pull them as tightly as possible so that you don't create air bubbles. Do the same at the top and repeat the process with the front cover fabric of the book. **D**

Finishing touches

5 Cut two pieces of embroidered paper that are just smaller than the book and glue them inside the front and back covers on top of the fabric edges. **E**

6 Trim the fabric strips that are created by the book binding, glue the edge and poke these into the hinge gap to secure. **F**

7 Stick trims along the edge of the book for a decorative finish and to hide any joinings. Cut two lengths of each to wrap around the entire length of the inside and outside cover. **G**

Tip

Ensure that the fabric is always pulled taut when you are gluing so that air bubbles do not get trapped. Keep smoothing it out using your hands – it will give your books a professional finish.

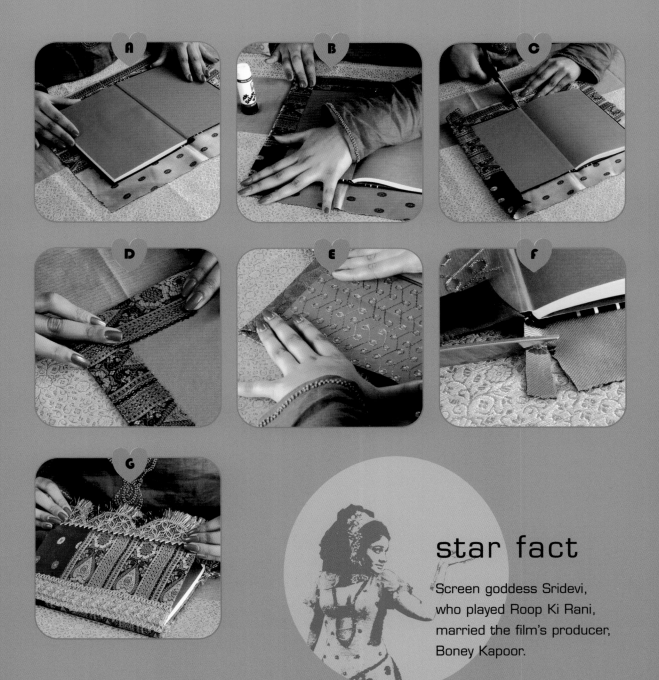

star fact

Screen goddess Sridevi, who played Roop Ki Rani, married the film's producer, Boney Kapoor.

2001

Khabi Khushi
Khabi Gham

Directed by Karan Johar

This is a traditional tale of family values, and it has become one of Bollywood's most successful movies of all time. Abbreviated to *K3G,* it focuses on the prosperous Raichand family empire, the head of which is played by Amitabh Bachchan, Bollywood's biggest movie star. In the film, his son Rahul falls in love with a lower caste girl, Anjali.

When Rahul is disowned for damaging the family honour by marrying her, the couple set up a new life in London. They are unaware when, years later, Rahul's younger brother, Rohan, becomes their lodger on a secret mission to reunite the family. The film is set in both India and the UK.

The movie's star-studded cast guaranteed the film's success. However, it is the catchy soundtrack and modern, original choreography that had the biggest impact on the viewer. The songs are frequent and all the dances are impressively shot. It is a fine example of how colourful and imaginative the musical elements of a Bollywood film are.

Khabi Khushi Khabi Gham is about 'happiness and tears', representing the emotions that families go through. There are several happy occasions, such as the father Yash's birthday, where the celebration bowl on page 97 would no doubt be useful.

When the main protagonists, Rahul and Anjali, move to London, they choose to live in a modern, suburban mansion. However, reminders of their life back in India prevail throughout their home in the form of décor and furniture – the vase on page 101 was designed especially for them.

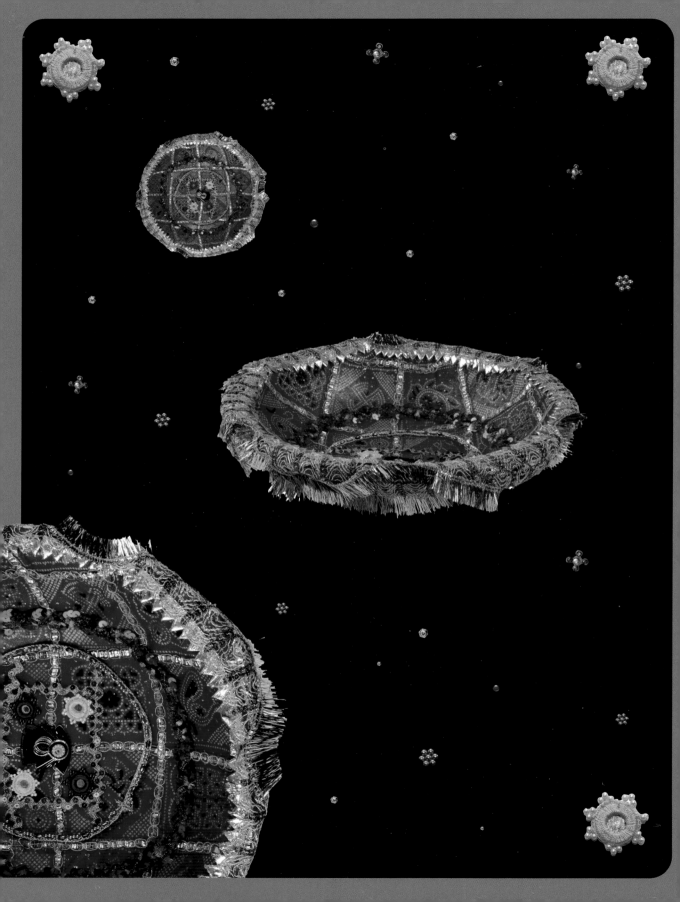

Celebration Bowl

Make these fabric-covered bowls to serve Indian sweets at a dinner party or fill with gifts and favours to give to wedding guests.

You will need:

Materials
* A round metal bowl
* Lightweight fabric of your choice (ensure there is enough to wrap around your bowl twice)
* Tinsel trim
* Thin sequin or beaded trims
* Ribbon trim
* Four shisha mirrors
* A small central motif
* PVA glue

Equipment
* Scissors
* Paintbrush

Covering the bowl

1 Apply PVA glue generously all over the inside of the bowl.

2 Push your fabric into the bowl so that it sticks down and lines the inside.

3 Use a paintbrush to pat the fabric into place and get rid of any folds or air bubbles; you won't be able to do this with your hands as it gets too sticky. Leave to dry overnight. **A**

4 Turn the bowl face down and then wrap the remaining fabric over the sides and at the bottom. You may need to trim it if it's too large. When you have enough fabric to completely cover the bowl, apply PVA glue all over the bottom of the bowl, as you did for the inside, and glue as before by pressing the fabric down with a dry paintbrush. You may need to add extra glue to affix any overlapping corners of fabric to secure in place. Leave to dry. **B**

5 Measure a length of tinsel trim to fit around the edge of the bowl.

6 Apply glue to the edge and then fix the trim in place. Use the brush to pat it down. **C**

Tip

It can be fiddly trying to get the fabric to stick inside the bowl; the trick is to use the large dry brush to keep patting out any air bubbles. You'll need to keep moving the brush around the entire bowl to ensure the whole fabric has stuck down properly. Don't attempt to glue the bottom of the bowl until the inner section is completely dry.

Decorating the bowl

7 Glue your motif in the middle. Create a box around it using ribbon trim and stick the four shisha mirrors in the corners. **D**

8 Finish by sticking two trims of your choice on the walls of the bowl. First measure them inside the bowl and cut them to size. Apply a line of PVA glue straight inside the bowl and then press the trims in place.

Tip

These bowls are not suitable for serving food but can be used to store wrapped favours.

Vase

If you're the sort of person who can't resist buying pretty trims whenever you visit a haberdashery then this easy vase project is a great way to put them to use.

You will need:

Materials
- A rectangular vase
- Fabric trims of your choice of varying widths
- Strong glue

Equipment
- Fabric scissors
- Glue applicator (optional)

1 Measure the trims you intend to use by wrapping them all around the vase. When you cut them to size make sure that you leave on an extra 2in (5cm) to allow for frays and for overlapping.

2 Work out the order in which you would like the trims to be on the vase. Remember that wider ribbons or trims should go underneath as it is easier to overlap with thinner trims.

3 Start from the bottom upwards, applying glue to the surface of the vase and all over each trim, especially at the ends. Wrap the trims around the vase and smooth out any air bubbles as you go. When the two ends meet, overlap them. Ensure all your trims overlap at the same place.

Tips

When choosing trims try to keep to ones that have a flat surface at the back. Trims that are heavily embroidered often have uneven backs and this makes them more difficult to stick down.

Make sure you start and finish each trim from the same place, as this will ensure that the joins are always at the back.

star fact

Amitabh and Jaya Bachchan, who play the Raichand family mother and father, are also married in real life.

2002

Devdas

Directed by Sanjay Leela Bhansali

This is the third remake of the influential Bengali novel of the same name by author Sarat Chandra Chattopadhay. The other versions were black and white and were released in 1935 and 1956. This version was, at the time, the most expensive Bollywood movie ever made. The sets, costumes and locations are exquisite, making the whole film very attractive to watch, which is a comfort since the storyline is so sad: the film follows the self-destruction of Devdas, a well-respected, educated man, into a lonely alcoholic.

For his whole life, Devdas (Shah Rukh Khan) is in love with his childhood sweetheart Paro (Aishwarya Rai). When his parents forbid him from marrying her, instead of standing up for himself, he allows Paro to be married off to an old man. His regret in loosing her haunts him, even when beautiful courtesan, Chandramukhi, falls in love with him. Rather than loving her back, he continues to torture himself by becoming ill from alcohol consumption.

While Devdas is away at college, Paro, played by former Miss World, Aishwarya Rai, keeps a candle alight. It burns continually until his return, many years later – it even burns when it comes in contact with rain. The candles on page 109 are inspired by this everlasting candle.

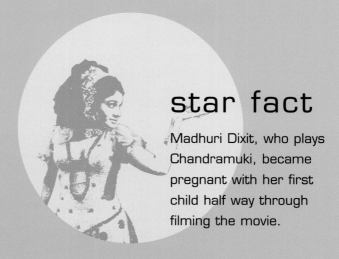

star fact

Madhuri Dixit, who plays Chandramuki, became pregnant with her first child half way through filming the movie.

As this is a classic movie with classic costumes, it seemed appropriate to create a project that would make use of traditional fabrics. On page 115, Indian-style fabrics have been converted into practical placemats that can be easily handwashed and used again and again.

Candles

If you enjoy painting, candles are an original way to display your designs. If you're not so keen on painting, you can still have a go at trying simple designs and shapes like these.

You will need:

Materials
- Plain cream candles
- Assorted gemstones, sequins and self-adhesive motifs
- Gold permanent marker pen
- Acrylic paints (water-based) and gold glitter acrylic paint
- Candle-painting medium
- Glitter liner
- White spirit
- Glue
- Pencil

Equipment
- Brushes: medium and fine
- Soft cloth

Preparing the candle surface

First wipe down each candle with a soft cloth dipped in white spirit. This will remove the manufacturer's finish that gives shop-bought candles their shiny appearance and will allow you to paint on the surface; if you don't remove it you'll find the candles resist the paint.

Painting the candle

Mix your paints with candle-painting medium to prevent the paint from cracking and to ensure they are easy to apply. To do this simply mix together equal parts of your paint colour and the medium. As the medium is white, you may find that it lightens the shade of your colour. If so, paint your first coat in this lighter shade then reduce the amount of medium for the second coat.

Blue candle

1 Paint the entire surface of the cream candle in blue. When dry apply a second coat.

2 Use a gold marker pen to draw a row of spots around the top and bottom. (A)

3 Draw a heart design in the centre. I drew one side of the heart continuously around the candle then drew the other side of the hearts afterwards to ensure neatness. (B)

4 Use the gold glitter paint to fill in the heart shapes and paint the top of the candle. (C)

Tips

✺ Do not burn these candles all the way down – just burn them enough to place a tealight in the well of the wick. When you wish to light the candles, all you need to do is keep replacing the tealights; this will preserve the designs.

✺ When you wipe down your candles with white spirit, do not be too vigorous as it can damage the candle by denting its surface.

✺ Although candle paints are available to purchase, there are no special ingredients that make them unique – acrylic paints mixed with a medium are just as effective.

5 Lastly, stick gemstones along the two ends and across the centre of the candle. (D)

Tips

🌼 The easiest way to paint the whole surface of a candle is to place it on a paper plate. This way you can move it around without touching the wet sides. If you place it on newspaper, it may stick to the bottom or leave newsprint marks.

🌼 You don't need to base your candle painting on the designs shown here: you can paint your candles any way you like and even transfer designs onto them using graphite transfer paper.

🌼 Each section of colour must be dried before painting the next to avoid smudging.

Yellow candle

1 Paint the entire candle with two coats of bright yellow.

2 Sketch your designs onto the candle with a pencil. Draw a star shape at the top of the candle, some large triangles across the top and bottom and a zigzag line.

3 Paint your shapes as shown using red and green. Again you will need to apply two coats of paint. When the candle is completely dry, outline the shapes using a gold marker pen. 🖤

4 Finish by sticking on various gems and motifs of your choice. 🖤

Tall candle

1 Using a variety of colours, paint stripes across the surface of the candle. You could use one colour several times, such as using the green paint for three stripes and making one stripe thicker than the others. Again, paint two coats of each. 🖤

2 When the stripes are dry, separate them using a glitter liner. Paint some of the stripes with a layer of glitter paint and, as before, stick on gems and motifs of your choice. You can also add any other shapes or motifs using acrylic paint, like the orange shapes. 🖤

Placemats

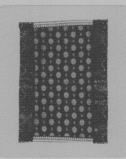

Bring a true flavour of India to your dinner table with these fabric placemats – perfect for serving with a home-cooked curry!

You will need:

Materials
- Fabrics and trims of your choice
- Threads to match and for tacking

Equipment
- Scissors
- Needle
- Sewing machine (optional)
- Dressmaking pins

Making the placemat

1 Before you begin, iron all your fabrics to remove any creases.

2 For each placemat you need two pieces of fabric that measure the same size. These should be 17½in (44.5cm) by 11½in (29cm) (this includes a ½in (1.5cm) seam allowance around all the sides).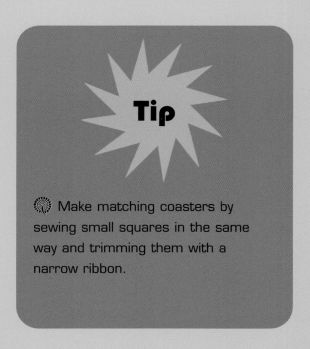

3 Put the right sides together and pin along the two horizontal edges and one vertical edge, ½in (1.5cm) in from the edge to create a pouch. Remove the pins and replace with tacking. Stitch all along the tacked lines and then remove the tacking.

4 Turn the fabric inside. Smooth out the centre to remove any trapped air and stitch down the remaining edge.

Attaching the trim edging

5 Cut two pieces of fabric trim exactly twice the length of the shorter edges of the placemat.

6 Fold one in half and pin it down the back and front of one of the short edges of the placemat. Do the same to the opposite edge. Stitch a line of tacking, remove the pins and then stitch them down.

7 Cut two trims for the long edges. This time cut them so that they are 1in (2.5cm) longer at either side. Pin, tack and then stitch them in place.

8 Fold the edge of the trims over onto the back and with small stitches sew them down – the end result should look discreet.

Tip

Make matching coasters by sewing small squares in the same way and trimming them with a narrow ribbon.

chorus

Mere piya ab aaja re mere piya
Ho, mere piya ab aaja re mere piya

**Come now, come to me
My love, come my love**

2003

Koi Mil Gaya

Directed by Rakesh Roshan

Science fiction and Bollywood may not be a common concoction, but this is the most successful Bollywood sci-fi movie ever made. It stars heart-throb actor Hritik Roshan as Rohit Mehra, whose late father was a scientist obsessed with making contact with extra-terrestrial life. Rohit is intrigued by his father's work after stumbling across his old computer and, without realising it, he and his friend Nisha soon find themselves in the company of a cute blue alien. This is Bollywood's take on the classic Hollywood production *ET* and could be described as 'Bollywood for children'.

The projects included here take inspiration from the idea of Bollywood meeting sci-fi. I've given them a silver and sparkly feel and used star-printed fabrics and sequins so they are reminiscent of the night sky. The bolster is a classic Indian soft furnishing and would be great for a child's bedroom with a space theme. The canvas project is all about letting your imagination run wild. It involves taking a plain canvas and an assortment of silvery trims and embellishments to create an individual piece of modern art.

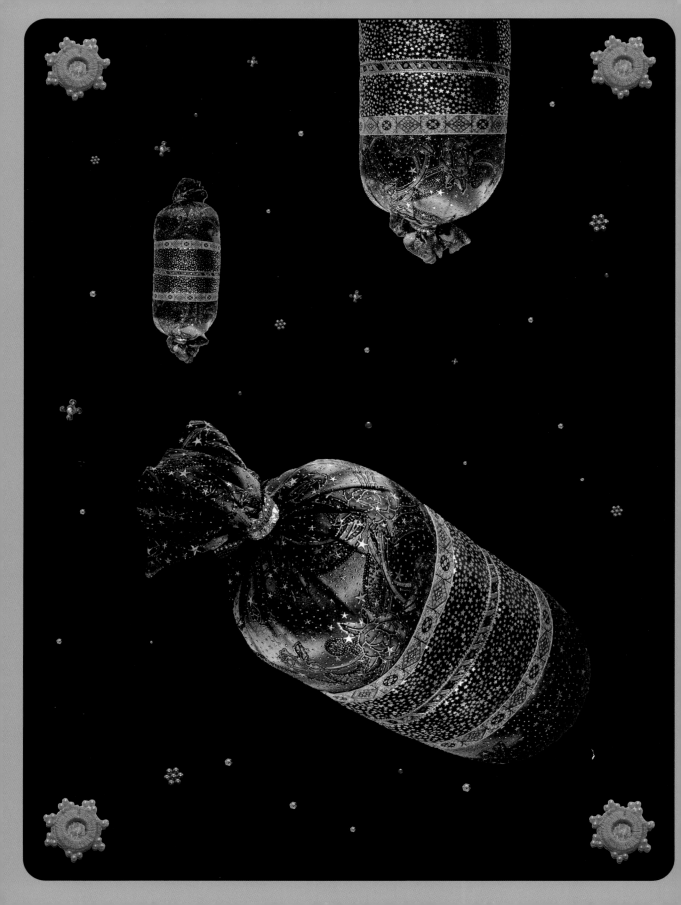

Bolster Cushion

Bolsters are an essential accessory for the Indian home. Place them on your bed for added luxury or on your sofas to lean against when reading, watching a movie or crafting!

You will need:

Materials
- A plain bolster cushion
- 3ft (1m) of your chosen sci-fi fabric and matching thread
- $9^1/_2$in (25cm) of a second fabric
- $6^1/_2$ft (2m) silver fabric trim
- Trims for bolster ends
- Elastic bands

Equipment
- Scissors
- Needle
- Pins

Wrapping the bolster

1 Lay the bolster in the centre of the fabric and then wrap the fabric around it, overlapping the edges. 🖤A

2 Gather and secure the fabric at each end with elastic bands. 🖤B

3 With a simple prick stitch (see page 144), sew up the fabric join. Take care not to stitch into the bolster cushion itself. 🖤C

4 Tie some trims of your choice around each end to disguise the elastic bands. 🖤D

star fact

Hritik Roshan is the son of the director, Rakesh Roshan. They are set to release a sequel to the movie called *Krrish*, Bollywood's first superhero movie.

Tips

🌸 Bolsters should be made in pairs so make sure you have a couple!

🌸 Most fabric will work for this project – why not try a soft fleecy fabric that will feel extra special to snuggle up against?

Centre section

5 Cut a rectangle of your second fabric so that it wraps once around the centre of the bolster with a 1in (2.5cm) overlap where the ends join. Pin this in the centre of the bolster and hand-stitch in place. Remove the pins. 🖤E

6 Cut two pieces of trim that fit on the edges of the middle section and hand-stitch in place. Cut another piece of trim and hand-stitch down the middle. 🖤F

Canvas Artwork

One of the easiest ways to make your own piece of modern art is to decorate a canvas. Use paint, fabric and any other embellishments you have at home to make something that is unique and personal.

You will need:

Materials
- A deep-edge canvas
- Silver spray paint
- Trims of your choice
- Star-print fabric
- Embellishments of your choice: bindis, sequins, stickers, motifs and anything else with a sci-fi/spacey feel
- Double-sided tape
- Glue

Equipment
- Scissors

Filling the background

1 Spray the entire canvas silver. Don't worry about being even; the more uneven your spraying, the more textured and interesting the background will be. Don't forget to spray the four sides, too. **A**

2 The canvas is split into two separate areas: trims and embellishments. Glue a rectangle of star fabric down the left-hand side of the canvas for the trim side. **B**

Adding the details

3 Cut lengths of trim that wrap all around the canvas, stick them on using double-sided tape so that the edges wrap right around the back edges of the canvas. **C**

4 For the right-hand side, stick on rows of different embellishments at an angle, such as sequins, bindis and stickers, until the surface is covered in rows. **D**

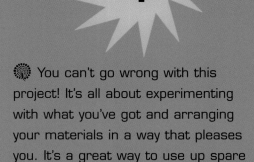

Tip

You can't go wrong with this project! It's all about experimenting with what you've got and arranging your materials in a way that pleases you. It's a great way to use up spare sequins and scraps of trims.

star fact

In *Krrish*, Hritik plays Rohit's son, who inherits superhero powers. Viewers can expect big-budget special effects and Matrix-style stunts.

Project
Preparation

Materials

It is always a good idea to have some basic craft materials to hand. They all have so many uses, from helping you whip up a quick birthday card for a friend or for creating larger-scale projects.

I have also compiled separate lists of useful extras and Bollywood materials. The Bollywood materials list includes the types of things you should be looking out for to make the projects in this book.

Basic materials

Glue

First and foremost, make sure that you always have a large bottle of PVA glue – it's the cleanest, safest and most easily obtained adhesive and has literally hundreds of uses! Stronger, tackier PVA-based glues are also worth having for when you need to glue stronger materials. For a stronger adhesive, mosaic or superglue are also necessary.

Pencils/pens

You can never have too many of these when you are crafting! You'll need both for when you are measuring fabrics or drawing on designs and motifs. Gelly roll or inky pens are good for drawing on felt and an HB pencil is sufficient for leaving faint marks on most fabrics.

Newspaper

Don't put all your newspaper in with the recycling – it comes in useful for almost all crafting projects and is a good way to protect your worktop, so always make sure you have an edition to hand.

Double-sided tape

Probably the most versatile and reliable of materials, so always make sure you have a roll at home. Double-sided tape is especially good for sticking down fabric trims; glue is too messy and leaves a hard finish.

Felt 🄓

Felt is cheap and easy to use because it doesn't fray. It's available in lots of different colours and textures, and it feels lovely to touch. It is made from pressed wool.

Beads 🄔

You will need small seed beads, round wooden beads and a selection of larger beads. Beads can be obtained from haberdasheries, but if you are able to visit a specialist bead shop you will find plenty of inspiration and be amazed by the variety available.

Ribbons 🄕

There are infinite uses for ribbons, so it's worth making sure you've always got some in stock. The variety on the market is huge – choose colours and designs that appeal to you.

Sequins/sequin trims 🄖

The best-known sequins are round, cupped shapes, but these days there is an amazing variety of shapes and designs available in the shops. Try to have different sizes and colours of round sequins, plus shaped ones, such as stars, and anything else unusual that you might like to use. Sequin trims are also a vital material for Bollywood crafting, as they provide instant professional results. Holed sequins are suitable for stitching onto fabrics but you can also get sequins without holes that can be attached with glue.

Jewels and gemstones 🄗

You'll need these in various shapes and sizes. Coloured acrylic gems are cheap and can usually be ordered from your local bead suppliers in any colour; some shops will dye them to your specification. The best-quality gems are Swarovski crystals. They have an incredible shine, making them glisten like diamonds! The only downside is that they are much more pricey, but if you want perfection in your crafts and you don't mind splashing out, you will definitely enjoy working with them.

Feathers 🄘

Dyed feathers are cheap and readily available from most craft stores. They are a lot of fun to use but be aware that little is known about the manufacturing of feathers. If you or your friends are concerned about how the feathers have been obtained, always seek assurance that birds have not been harmed in the process.

Acrylic paints

These are versatile and give a good coverage. Acrylic paints can be applied to many surfaces and have been used in all the painting projects here. Use water-based acrylics as it makes it easier to clean your hands and brushes. Rather than buying small tubes, it's worth investing in larger bottles of white and the three primary colours, red, blue and yellow, so that you can mix shades and colours of your choice. Gold and silver acrylic paints will also be useful.

Glitter

Glitter always adds sparkle and glamour, and can be used to jazz up almost any craft project. It is available in so many versions now that it means you can have glitter in all aspects of your life; from glittery furniture paint to glittery fabrics – there's no escaping the sparkly stuff! For these projects you'll just need some fine glitter dust but don't be afraid to use it in any of the projects to suit your tastes.

Yarn

Yarn has a wealth of uses, and not just for knitters. Try using unusual yarns to make tassels. Tapestry yarn is thicker and will create a much bigger tassel.

Thread

There are several projects of a sewing nature that require the use of thread. For the most professional finish always use a thread that matches the colour of your fabric. If you intend to use a sewing machine, 'sewing machine threads' are worth investing in as they are less likely to tear than some of the cheaper threads.

Useful extras

Glue gun and glue sticks

If the materials you use are heavy a glue gun is worth investing in as it adheres woods and metals. There are no specific projects here that require a glue gun, but as they are quite affordable you may want to buy one for your craft toolbox.

Tailor's chalk

If you are a dressmaker you may already have some of this at home. It is a chalk made especially for drawing on fabrics and rubs off easily. You may find it easier to use than drawing pen lines on your fabrics.

Fabric glue

If you are not a fan of sewing then fabric glue can be substituted for some fabric-based projects, such as gluing the appliqué cushion on page 59. However, there are several fabric glues on the market, so make sure that you buy one that is suited to the fabric you wish to use – don't use PVA as it will cause the fabric to harden.

Tracing paper/carbon copy paper

Tracing paper is needed to transfer basic designs and motifs, and can be used with carbon copy paper to transfer a design onto any surface, such as wood or candle wax. None of these projects require templates; however, if you are adjusting any of the projects you may find that you need to trace templates of shapes or patterns.

White spirit

Although not essential, you can keep your brushes clean by using white spirit. You will also need some kind of household cleaning alcohol for the candle-painting project on page 109 in order to clean the candle surface before you start.

Bollywood materials

Bindis and stickers Ⓐ

Bindis, although traditionally used as face/body ornaments, also make good alternatives to stickers, especially for paper-crafting. You can make them permanent on other crafts by adding extra glue to their adhesive side.

Fabric trims Ⓑ

Whether they are beaded, gold, tinselled or woven, the quickest way to achieve the Bollywood look is with the addition of Indian fabric trims. Although most haberdashery stores now stock a variety of trims, many sari and Indian-fabric shops also sell trims, and they are usually much cheaper.

Clothing/garments Ⓒ

If you have any clothes with Indian-inspired prints or designs that you don't mind cutting up and immortalizing in your craftwork, then these materials can also be used for projects. A good place to look is charity shops; you may find oversized clothes made from good-quality fabrics.

Indian fabrics Ⓓ

You'll need several printed fabrics of different thicknesses. There's no harm in picking up fabrics from your local haberdashery shop but for the most authentic look it's well worth tracking down an Indian clothing specialist for real Indian fabrics. You'll be amazed at what you find – there will be no shortage of inspiration.

Shisha mirrors Ⓔ

Iconic in terms of Indian craftwork and textiles, these are the small mirrors that sit in their own embroidered borders and will guarantee an 'ethnic' theme to your work. They aren't made of mirrors as such, but tend to be silver sequins or foils that go underneath a separate embroidered frame.

Motifs Ⓕ

You may come across Indian-themed iron-on motifs, such as elephants or paisley shapes, stickers or other fabric or paper motifs. They have a wide range of uses in crafting.

Embroidered paper

The popularity of ready-made embroidered papers is on the increase and they should be available from your local art and craft store. You can also make your own embroidered paper if you are confident with a sewing machine.

Scarves

Indian silk scarves look stunning worn, but also when cut up and used in your crafting. Substitute them for any of the fabric projects.

Decorations

Some Indian stores stock magnificent party decorations, such as floral wreaths, gold placemats or hangings. Any of these things can be incorporated into your own crafts.

Equipment

There are two types of equipment you should aim to have: basic tools, which are the essentials and are commonly available, and useful extras, which are worth investing in if you intend to do a lot of crafting. Keeping them together in your own craft box means you'll always know where they are, which saves time when you're making things.

Basic kit

Brushes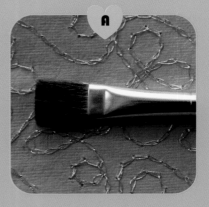

Don't be tempted to buy a cheap set, as the bristles tend to fall off and might ruin your work. You will need a fine brush for painting details, a medium-size brush for applying paint to larger surface areas and a large brush that can be used as a dry implement for patting and holding things down. Wash your brushes after each use, as they are much easier to clean than when old paint has dried on them.

Scissors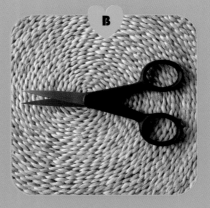

You will need several pairs for doing different jobs. Try not to use scissors that have become sticky through cutting tape – instead, keep pairs for different purposes. It's worth having a small pair for cutting details on paper, a larger pair for cutting larger papers, a non-stick pair for when you do have to cut sticky things, such as tape, and a good-quality pair for cutting fabrics. Keep scissors clean by regularly wiping them down with wet wipes.

Craft knife and mat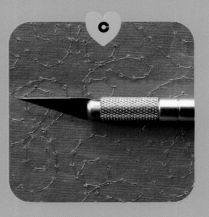

Craft knives often do a job better than scissors, as you can get around curves and make finer edges, especially if you are cutting card. Always place anything you are cutting on a craft mat so that you don't damage your work surface. If you are cutting shapes that are particularly curvy, a scalpel with a thin blade may be more effective.

Needles and pins ⓓ

You will need an ordinary-size needle for when you are doing simple hand-stitches with thread and a narrower bead needle. Dressmaking pins are also vital for the fabric-based projects to hold fabrics in place.

Ruler

A transparent ruler will ensure your lines are aligned accurately, especially when you are measuring fabric. Metal rulers are useful for cutting against.

Glue spreader ⓔ

A plastic glue spreader, like the ones you used at school, will make your life easier when you are applying glue.

Cocktail sticks ⓕ

Have some cocktail sticks to hand too, as these are good for when you are gluing fine details.

Useful extras

Sewing machine

The sewing projects in this book can be done by hand-stitching but a sewing machine will certainly speed up the process. If you know how to use one, you should definitely own one and if you don't know, then ask someone to teach you or attend a class. Once you have sewn on a machine you'll never look back!

Iron

You'll need an iron to press your fabrics before you use them. This will ensure a professional finish and make the fabric easier to handle. An iron is also required for melting fusible webbing – a bonding agent that is used to fix hems and is particularly suited to thin, delicate fabrics such as saris.

Tweezers

These are useful when handling small items, such as gemstones or beads, which are too fiddly to use fingers for. Ensure you only lift them loosely and do not apply too much pressure, as you may damage the gemstone.

Needle unpicker A

This is a small tool that is a must for sewers. It can be used to unpick any stitches you've made that have gone wrong by cutting through them without damaging your work. It's far more accurate than trying to unstitch something with scissors or other sharp items. If you enjoy sewing but often make mistakes, like sewing wonky lines, it's worth having one.

Lamp

It is always advisable to work in a well-lit area but an extra lamp shone over your workspace will help you see better – some craft stores sell specific lamps with small but powerful bulbs especially made for crafting.

Techniques

There are lots of techniques used in this book, from sewing to painting. You may be confident at some and have not yet tried others but don't be put off: all are easily explained so that anyone can have a go. Often you may already have your own way of doing a particular technique, perhaps a method you learnt as a child or have seen a friend do. However, if you do get stuck, turn to this section to remind yourself of everything you need to know.

Sewing

These projects are all suitable for hand-stitching, but if you can use a sewing machine you will find some projects, such as the placemats, quicker to make.

For basic hand-stitching you need a needle, thread and scissors, and if you have problems threading a needle, it may be worth buying a needle-threader to make it easier for you.

Pin and tack

Most projects will say to 'pin and tack' the fabric before you sew it. This will make your sewing more accurate and refers to a temporary stitch before adding your final sewing stitch.

1 Hold your two fabrics together, leave a $\frac{1}{2}$in (1.5cm) gap from the edge and place your pins in a straight line across the fabric. **A**

2 Next you need to tack them. Thread a needle in a colour that is easily visible, such as a contrasting colour. Tie a knot at one end and make quick, loose stitches in a straight line as close to the pins as you can get. This will create a simple running stitch. Once you have completed the tacking, you do not need to tie it off but you should remove the pins ready for the next stage. **B**

3 Once you remove the pins your tacking will be holding your work in place. You can now do your proper line of stitching directly on the tacking line or a millimetre or so away from it. When your stitching is complete, carefully cut the tacking thread out – because it is a loose stitch, it will be easy to remove. **C**

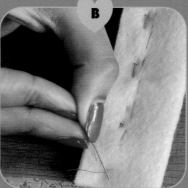

Prick stitch ⓓ

This is the stitch I've used for most of the sewing projects. It is a tiny hand-stitch that is so small it seems invisible from the front side of the work. It works best if your thread colour matches your fabric so that it is discretely disguised. The front stitches will look like tiny pricks while the reverse side of your work will look like an even-spaced running stitch.

Couching ⓔ

This helps you stitch a trim in place and is especially suited to stitching down sequin trims. You simply stitch on top of the stitches of the trim, underneath each sequin so that the stitches are hidden but the sequins become attached to the fabric.

Running stitch ⓕ

This is the most basic stitch used to attach two pieces of fabric together. It involves sewing in a straight line making even-spaced stitches so that the front and back look the same.

Gluing ⓖ

When gluing small things, like gemstones, apply the glue directly to the middle back of the gem using a cocktail stick. That way you won't get sticky fingers, and when it is pressed into place the glue won't spread over the sides. If glue does spread out from underneath – don't panic! PVA dries clear but if you are worried, fold a piece of tissue so that it has a sharp point and wipe the glue away.

Cutting with a craft knife

First of all make sure you do any cutting on top of a cutting mat. If the piece you are cutting out is larger than your mat, move it along so that you always cut directly on the mat. It is often easier to work on the floor but don't bend your back for too long. To get a smooth, even cut, keep the blade as flat as possible and remember to change blades regularly, as they do get blunt.

Spraying paint

If possible, always spray outside, as you need to be in a well-ventilated space. If you are spraying indoors, always open windows and doors. Lay lots of newspaper on the floor and then place your piece on top. Stand about 12in (30cm) away and spray all over your piece in an even manner. For a more uneven effect, spray some areas more than others.

Glitter

If you are using glitter, lay down newspaper on your work surface and then try and work directly over some plain paper. Glue your area, sprinkle on the glitter directly from its container and then leave to dry overnight. Shake the excess glitter off onto the plain paper. You can then fold the paper in half, make a really sharp fold, and pour it back into the original container so that the extra glitter can be used again.

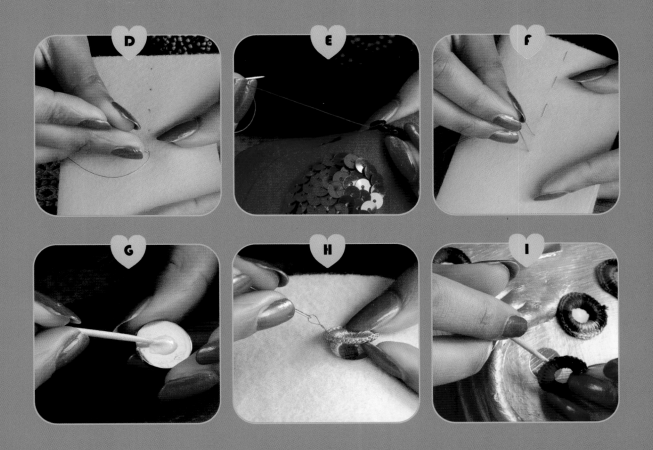

Attaching shisha mirrors

If you are sewing a shisha mirror onto fabric, place the mirror foil where you want it to go, place the frame on top and stitch through the frame onto the fabric so that the foil is secured.

If you are gluing the shisha mirrors on, first place a tiny bit of glue on the centre back of the foil using a cocktail stick or fine brush then glue in place. Next glue the border surface and place directly on top. You will only need a thin layer; if it's too heavy the glue will spread on to the surface of the foil. If this happens, leave it to dry; it should be clear if you used PVA but if it isn't, use a damp tissue to clean it up.

Safety Notes

Although crafting is a lot of fun, you will encounter equipment and tools that need to be handled with care to keep yourself and everyone around you safe. Make sure you follow the advice opposite.

Scissors

Always cut away from yourself so that the sharp blades cannot come in contact with you. It is best to store scissors in a scissor pouch if you have one.

Craft knife

Always work on a craft mat. If you are cutting against a ruler, only use a metal one to protect your fingers as the blade can cut through plastic rulers. When not in use, keep the blades retracted, and do not use blunt blades as these can be unpredictable – they won't cut well and are more likely to move around.

Needles and pins

Keeping your pins and needles in a pincushion makes them easy to access and means you don't lose them on the floor. If you don't have one, you could fold a piece of felt into a rectangle wrap and store your pins by pinning them into the felt.

Sewing machine

If you are using a sewing machine, there are several factors that you need to consider. Keep water/children/pets away from electricals. Make sure the mains plug and lead is properly fitted and tucked away so that it doesn't trip anybody up.

Ventilation

When using spray paints, white spirit, strong glues and permanent marker pens, make sure you work in well ventilated areas. You can either leave your doors or windows open or work outside. Anything that is solvent-based should not be directly breathed in.

Adhesives

PVA glue is the safest glue to use, as it is non-toxic and washable so especially suited for children. There are some projects that require stronger glues, such as superglue; use these with care – try not to get them on your fingers. Always read manufacturer's instructions regarding use and storage.

General

If you are doing any kind of craftwork, you must have sufficient lighting. Never attempt to craft in the dark. You can often focus on a task, such as hand-stitching, for a long period of time, so make sure you don't strain your eyes by working in poor light. A lamp in addition to natural or ceiling lighting usually helps. However, just as you need screen breaks when using a computer, don't 'over-craft'! Remember to take regular breaks from whatever you're doing. This will also improve your craftwork, as looking at a project with fresh eyes helps you see where it can be improved.

Suppliers

To make these projects you will need to obtain materials from two types of store or online supplier: general arts and craft shops and Indian fabric stores.

General art and craft

UK

1st For Crafts
South Street
Braintree
Essex
CM7 3HA
www.1stforcrafts.com
Email: email@1stforcrafts.com
Tel: +44 (0)1376 550099
Fax: +44 (0)1376 551177
For sequins, paper, cards, beads, glitter and feathers

Barnett, Lawson (Trimmings) Ltd
16/17 Little Portland Street
London
W1W 8NE
www.bltrimmings.com
Tel: +44 (0)207 636 8591
Fax: +44 (0)207 7850 0069
For every kind of trim imaginable, motifs, buttons and feathers

Creative Beadcraft (Ells and Farrier)
20 Beak Street
London
W1F 9RE
www.creativebeadcraft.co.uk
Email: tracy@ellso707.co.uk
Tel: +44 (0)207 629 9964
For beads, sequins, gemstones and Swarovski crystals. They also dye acrylic stones to your chosen colour

Fred Aldous
37 Lever Street
Manchester
M1 1LU
www.fredaldous.co.uk
Email: aldous@btinternet.com
Tel: +44 (0)8707 517301
Fax: +44 (0)8707 517303
For adhesives, beads, sequins, paints, scissors, pens and pencils

Glitterati Handicrafts Ltd

Email: glitterati2001@aol.com

Tel: +44 (0)208 208 2232

For the biggest supply of shisha mirrors, Indian motifs, stickers, craft accessories and trims. Email your requests directly to them and they can send items out

Hobbycraft

(Stores nationwide)

www.hobbycraft.co.uk

Call free on +44 (0)800 027 2387

An art and craft superstore with over 32,000 products for all your crafting needs, including large bottles of PVA, felt and candle-painting medium

Ikea

www.ikea.com

For items to transform, such as frames, mirrors, vases and pots

Papercellar

www.papercellar.com

Email: contact@papercellar.com

Tel: +44 (0)208 426 1555

For embroidered papers and stickers – the 'make it yourself complements' range is particularly good and was used for the Bindi Card project

Paperchase

www.paperchase.co.uk

Tel: +44 (0)207 467 6200

For card and embroidered paper

The Works

www.theworks.gb.com

Tel: +44 (0)121 3136000

Fax: +44 (0)121 3136001

Email: cs@theworks.gb.com

For canvases, brushes, paints and sequins

AUSTRALIA

Australian Craft Network Pty Ltd

PO Box 350

Narellan

NSW 2567

Tel: +61 (02) 4648 5053

Fax: +61 (02) 8572 8256

Email: admin@auscraftnet.co.au

www.auscraftnet.com

For general art and craft materials

CANADA

Lewiscraft

www.lewiscraft.ca

A large selection of art and craft materials

USA

CraftAmerica.com
498 Dreyfus Road
Berea
KY 40403
Tel: +1 877 306 9178
info@craftamerica.com
www.craftamerica.com
For beads. brushes and paper

Crafts, etc!
(Domestic) Tel: 1806 888 0321
(International) Tel: +1 405 745 1200
www.craftsetc.com
*For brushes, paints, canvas, candles
and adhesives*

Papercellar LLC
550 Kane Ct.
Suite 100
Ovledo
FL 32765
www.papercellar.com
Tel: +1 800 805 0818
For embroidered papers and stickers

Indian fabrics

UK   **There are Indian areas throughout the UK, especially within larger cities, such as Manchester and Birmingham, which will have shops that stock Indian fabrics. I obtained all my Indian fabrics and materials from Green Street in East London and Southall in West London. Both areas make fantastic daytrips if you like browsing stunning fabrics and bright colours. You will also pick up inspiration and have the opportunity to purchase Bollywood CDs and DVDs.**

New Rainbow Textiles Ltd
98 The Broadway
Southall
Middlesex
UB1 1QF
Tel: +44 (0)208 574 1494
For saris and fabrics

Partap
202–206 Green Street
Forest Gate
London
E7 8LE
www.partapfashions.com
Email: enquiries@partapfashions.com
Tel: +44 (0)208 472 2157
For saris, fabrics and trims imported
from India

Party 4 U
33 Green Street
Forest Gate
London
E7 8DA
Tel: +44 (0)208 471 4957
For decorations and motifs

The Button Shop (J.R. Tailors)
87 Green Street
London
E7 8JF
Tel: +44 (0)208 552 5727
For Indian trims, motifs and sequins

 Indian fabrics: INTERNATIONAL MAIL ORDER

Indian Sky Ltd
www.indiansky.com
Email: cs@indiansky.com
Tel: +44 (0)208 946 3680
For saris, scarves and shawls

Kaneesha Boutique
www.kaneesha.com
USA Tel: 732 662 7519
UK Tel: 0207 669 4341
Australia Tel: 613 808 03110

Further Recommended Viewing

So many fantastic films have been made throughout Bollywood history that it's difficult to select a few to recommend. In particular I love the kitsch and colourful films that were made through the sixties and seventies. The selection of films I have chosen here are all modern-day classics from recent years. They are easy to obtain and between them all represent aspects that really show Bollywood at its best. I hope you will enjoy watching them and the ten other films that this book has taken inspiration from.

Black
Director: Sanjay Leela Bhansali (2005)
A departure from traditional Bollywood, this is a drama with no songs, dance or spectacle. It follows the life of a deaf, blind and mute girl and how she appreciates life with the help of her teacher.

Jism
Director: Amit Saxena (2003)
A psychological adult thriller about deceit and seduction that will have you gripped!

Kal Ho Naa Ho
Director: Nikhil Advani (2003)
Emotional US set drama that taps into all your senses; you'll need to watch this with a tissue box beside you.

Lagaan
Director: Ashutosh Gowarikar (2001)
Oscar-nominated historical epic following heroic villagers as they take up the challenge to play the most important cricket match of their lives – it features a British cast.

Main Hoo Na

Director: Farah Khan (2004)

Bollywood multi-genre at its best, this movie mixes fun comedy performances with a shocking action-packed plot.

Monsoon Wedding

Director: Mira Nair (2002)

Although an English-language movie, this is a brilliant portrayal of modern-day India which is visually stunning with a storyline that is memorable and highly watchable.

Paheli

Director: Amol Palekha (2005)

A fun children's story based on Indian folklore tales and told through the eyes of puppets.

Rang De Basanti

Director: Rakesh Omprakash Mehra (2006)

Delhi University is the setting where a group of young students volunteer to be part of a docu-drama about Indian Freedom fighters. They become aware of the issues that were faced by their ancestors and soon become caught up in their own political causes.

Taxi Number 9211

Director: Milan Luthria (2006)

Shot and set entirely in Mumbai, this story follows one day in the life of a taxi driver and a wealthy socialite. It is captivating viewing and has a refreshingly unpredictable storyline.

Veer-Zaara

Director: Yash Chopra (2004)

A tragic love story between an Indian army officer and a Pakistani girl and the political issues that arise due to their relationship.

Acknowledgements

I would like to thank the following people for their help and support whilst writing this book. Thank you to Hobbycraft and Coats Crafts UK for donating materials, the staff at GMC Publications for believing in my book, Nasreen Munni Kabir for her advice, Yash Raj Films and Roli Books for help in obtaining film stills, Indian Book Shelf, London, for supplying DVDs, Mr Matt Ponting for IT expertise and my family for everything, especially great lunches.

Momtaz Begum-Hossain and GMC Publications would like to thank the following people for the use of their film stills:

Awara © RK Film Studios, supplied courtesy of Yash Raj Films: p.14, pp.16–17

Bobby © RK Film Studios, supplied courtesy of Yash Raj Films: back cover (top), p.12, p.62, p.128

Caravan © Nasir Hussain Films, supplied courtesy of *Indian Cinema: The Bollywood Saga* by Dinesh Raheja and Jitendra Kothari, published by Roli Books, 2004: front cover (left), p.8, p.50

Devdas © Mega Bollywood Pvt., supplied courtesy of Eros International/Hyphen Films Collection: front cover (right), p.6 (right), p.104 and p.107

Jewel Thief © Navketan International Films, supplied courtesy of Hyphen Films Collection/Navketan: p.38, p.41

Khabi Khushi Khabi Gham © Dharma Productions, supplied courtesy of Dharma Productions: p.7 (top), p.92, p.95

Koi Mil Gaya © Filmkraft Productions Pvt. Ltd., supplied courtesy of Filmkraft Productions Pvt. Ltd.: back cover (bottom), p.118

Mughal-E-Azam © Sterling Investment Corporation Pvt. Ltd., supplied courtesy of Hyphen Films Collection/Sterling Corporation: p.8, p.50

Roop Ki Rani Choron Ka Raja © Narsimha Enterprises, supplied courtesy of *Indian Cinema: The Bollywood Saga* by Dinesh Raheja and Jitendra Kothari, published by Roli Books, 2004: p.7 (bottom), p.82

Umrao Jaan © Kotwara Studios, supplied courtesy of Hyphen Films Collection: p.6 (bottom left), p.72

About the Author

Momtaz Begum-Hossain is a crafts journalist who has written for and edited *Popular Crafts* magazine and made crafts for children's publications including *Crafts For Children*, *Crazy Crafts* and several BBC children's and pre-school magazines. She can be contacted at **www.momtazbh.co.uk**. This is her first book.

Index

A

acrylic paints 110, 133
actors 10–11
adhesives see
glues/adhesives
Advani, Nikhil 152
air bubbles 54, 90, 98
Ali, Muzaffar 73
Anand, Dev 40
Anand, Vijay 38
artwork, canvas 119, 124–7
Asif, K. 27
Awara 9, 14–17
sari bedspread 17, 22–5
silver mirror 17, 18–21

B

Bachchan, Amitabh 93, 102
Bachchan, Jaya 102
beaded trim 86, 87
beads 32, 44, 132, 133
hanging on sandals 70, 71
string of 80
bedspread, sari 17, 22–5
belt 73, 74–7
Bhansali, Sanjay Leela
105, 152
bindi greeting card 64–7
bindis 136, 137
Black 152
blue candle 110–11

Bobby 62–3
bindi greeting card 64–7
sandals 68–71
Bollywood films 10–11,
152–3
see also under each
individual film
bolster cushion 119, 120–3
bowl, celebration 96–9
brooches 40, 42–5
brushes 139
bugle beads 32

C

candle-painting medium 110
candle paints 110
candles 106, 108–13
canvas artwork 119, 124–7
Caravan 50–1
cushion 51, 58–61
lamp 51, 52–7
carbon copy paper 135
celebration bowl 96–9
Chattopadhay, Sarat Chandra
105
Chopra, Yash 153
choreography 10
clothing 136, 137
coasters 116
cocktail sticks 32, 140
applying glue 36,
144, 145

patting down sequins
and gemstones 44
colour 40
costumes 51
couching 76, 80, 81,
144, 145
craft knife 139
cutting with 144
safety 147
craft mat 139, 144, 147
cushions
based on *Caravan* 51,
58–61
bolster 119, 120–3
cutting mat 139, 144, 147

D

decorations 136
Devdas 104–7
candles 106, 108–13
placemats 107, 114–17
Dixit, Madhuri 106
double-sided tape 131

E

embroidered paper 90,
91, 136
emotion, expression of 10
equipment 138–41
basic 139–40
useful extras 141

F

fabric
  covering a bowl 98, 99
  covering a lampshade 54
  covering a notebook
    90, 91
  gluing 90, 98
  Indian fabrics 136, 137
  wrapping a bolster
    cushion 122
  wrapping trinket boxes
    48, 49
fabric bags 86
fabric glue 86, 135
fabric trims 76, 136, 137
feathers 132, 133
felt 44, 60, 80, 81,
    132, 133
  plaque for sandals 70, 71
filling, cushion 60
fine glitter dust 32, 134
foam 48
fusible webbing 24, 141

G

garments 136, 137
gemstones 20, 32, 44, 54,
    132, 133
giant badge 44
glitter 32, 134
  using 144
glitter liner 112
glitter paint 112
glue gun 135

glue spreader 140
glue sticks 135
glues/adhesives 131
  fabric 86, 135
  mosaic 36, 131
  PVA 32, 98, 131, 135,
    144, 147
  safety 147
  superglue 70, 86,
    131, 147
gluing 144, 145
  fabric 90, 98
  sequins and gemstones
    etc 32, 44
  shisha mirrors 145
  trims 54
gold pot 29, 34–7
Gowarikar, Ashutosh 152
greeting card 64–7
grouting 36

H

handbag 84–7
Helen 56
Hindi 10
holed sequins 132, 133
Hussain, Nasir 51

I

Indian fabrics 136, 137
Irani, Aruni 54
iron 141

J

Jewel Thief 38–41
  brooches 40, 42–5
  trinket boxes 40, 46–9
jewels 132, 133
Jism 152
Johar, Karan 93

K

Kal Ho Naa Ho 152
Kapadia, Dimple 63, 71
Kapoor, Boney 91
Kapoor, Raj 14, 17, 21, 63
Kapoor, Rishi 63
Kaushik, Satish 83
Khabi Khushi Khabi Gham
    92–5
  celebration bowl 96–9
  vase 100–3
Khan, Farah 153
Khan, Shah Rukh 106
Koi Mil Gaya 9, 118–19
  bolster cushion 119,
    120–3
  canvas artwork 119,
    124–7
Krrish 122, 126

L

Lagaan 152
lamps
  based on *Caravan*
    51, 52–7

lighting for craft 141, 147
Luthria, Milan 153

M
Main Hoo Na 153
marabou trim 70, 71
materials 130–7
  basic 131–4
  Bollywood materials
    136–7
  useful extras 135
Mehra, Rakesh Omprakash
  153
mirrors
  shisha mirrors see shisha
    mirrors
  silver mirror 17, 18–21
Monsoon Wedding 153
mosaic 36
mosaic glue 36, 131
motifs 48, 98, 136, 137
Mughal-E-Azam 26–9
  gold pot 29, 34–7
  photo frame 29, 30–3

N
Nair, Mira 153
Nargis 17
neck purse 73, 78–81
needle threader 143
needle unpicker 141
needles 140
  safety 147
newspaper 131
notebooks 88–91

P
Paheli 153
painting
  candles 110, 112
  spray painting 126, 144
  wedges on sandals 70, 71
paints 110, 133
Palekha, Amol 153
paper plate 112
papier-mâché 20
party decorations 136
pencils 131
pens 131
photo frame 29, 30–3
pin badge 44
pin and tack 143
pins 140
  safety 147
placemats 107, 114–17
prick stitch 60, 80, 122,
  144, 145
purse 73, 78–81
PVA glue 32, 98, 131, 135,
  144, 147

R
Rai, Aishwarya 81, 106
Rang De Basanti 153
ribbons 76, 132, 133
Roop Ki Rani Choron Ka Raja
  82–3
  handbag 84–7
  notebooks 88–91
Roshan, Hritik 119,
  122, 126

Roshan, Rakesh 119, 122
ruler 140
running stitch 60, 144, 145

S
safety 146–7
sandals 68–71
sari bedspread 17, 22–5
Saxena, Amit 152
scalpel 139
scarves 136
scissors 139
  safety 147
seed beads 44
Selfridges 71
sequin trims 70, 76,
  132, 133
  couching 76, 80, 81
sequins 132, 133
  gluing 32, 44
  photo frame 29, 32–3
  sewing 76, 77
sewing 143–4
  sequins 76, 77
  shisha mirrors 76, 77,
    145
sewing machine 141
  safety 147
sewing machine threads 134
shisha mirrors 136, 137
  attaching 76, 77, 145
  gold pot 29, 36–7
silver mirror 17, 18–21
song sequences 10
spray painting 126, 144

Sridevi 91
stickers 66, 136, 137
superglue 70, 86, 131, 147
suppliers 148–51
Swarovski crystals 44, 133

T
tacking 143
tailor's chalk 135
tall candle 112, 113
tapestry yarn 134
tassels 56, 57
Taxi Number 9211 153
tealights 110
techniques 142–5
templates 135
thread 134
tinsel trim 98
tracing paper 135
trims
    beaded 86, 87
    edging placemats 116,
        117
    fabric trims 76, 136, 137
    flat backs 102
    gluing 54
    marabou 70, 71
    sequin trims see sequin
trims
trinket boxes 40, 46–9
tweezers 141

U
Umrao Jaan 72–3
    belt 73, 74–7
    neck purse 73, 78–81
    remake of 81

V
Veer-Zaara 153
velvet trim 76
ventilation 147

W
webbing, fusible 24, 141
wedge sandals 68–71
white spirit 110, 135

Y
yarn 134
yellow candle 112, 113

GMC Publications Ltd
Castle Place, 166 High Street,
Lewes, East Sussex, BN7 1XU
United Kingdom

Tel: 01273 488005
Fax: 01273 402866
E-mail: pubs@thegmcgroup.com
Website: www.gmcbooks.com

Contact us for a complete
catalogue, or visit our website.
Orders by credit card are
accepted.

The End